Dream Trip
to the Orient

© 2017 Katharine Salter Mahmood

All rights reserved. No part of this book may be reproduced or transmitted in any form or by any means, electronic or mechanical, or by any information or storage and retrieval system without permission in writing from the author or publisher.

Published by Compass Flower Press

an imprint of AKA-Publishing
Columbia, Missouri USA
www.AKA-Publishing.com

Trade Paper ISBN: 978-1-942168-82-9

Maps used in this book are not to scale.

Dream Trip
to the Orient

Katharine Salter Mahmood

In loving memory of Katharine, who lived her dreams and for Natalia who was her dream.

Foreword

As I re-read the brittle and yellowed onionskin pages of my mother Kate's writing from more than sixty years ago, many thoughts come to mind. The metaphor of onionskin typing paper seems so appropriate given the layers of intrigue and richness that characterized her *Mongolia* journey.

After graduating from Mills College in 1943, she worked for the Pentagon in Washington D.C. as researcher for the Office of War Information. She transferred to Germany in 1946, working at the Rhein-Main Air Force Base near Frankfurt. She covered the Berlin Airlift and wrote general stories related to the Allied Occupation. After leaving this post in December of 1949 she undertook her six-week voyage from Rotterdam to Manila. That voyage gave rise to this journal.

This poignant tale of a twenty-seven year old American woman is deeply moving. Due to the recent tragic plane crash resulting in the death of her fiancé, a Major in the U.S. Army, Kate became deeply despondent and eager to take a break from reality. In December 1949, she booked a small cabin on a Danish freighter, the MS *Mongolia*. She and eleven other passengers—along with a diverse cargo—made their way to the Far East over the next month and a half. Her heartwarming embrace of the eclectic mix of people she encountered, coupled with her capacity to deal with her recent loss, reveal the characteristic strength of her pioneering spirit.

This traveler's tale, presented as a continuous letter to her family and friends, is rich in texture and prose. The pages reveal the complexity of her living in Germany post-World War II, her personal heartache and loss compounded by her simultaneous euphoria and elation to be traveling to a fresh and exotic destination with such a multicultural and diverse group of passengers. Her enthusiasm and candor, mixed with humor and introspection, vividly portray this adventure. From Rotterdam to Manila, from ecstasy to tragedy, her tale paints a vibrant yet chaotic depiction of life at the turn of the decade on board the *Mongolia*. The added mysterious element of an Italian Princess "lying in state" within the hold of the ship adds to the journal's masala and intrigue.

The novelty of being an independent, beautiful young woman, traveling alone with virtually all of her life possessions on her "honeymoon for one," is a very moving chronicle.

Kashya Mahmood Hildebrand

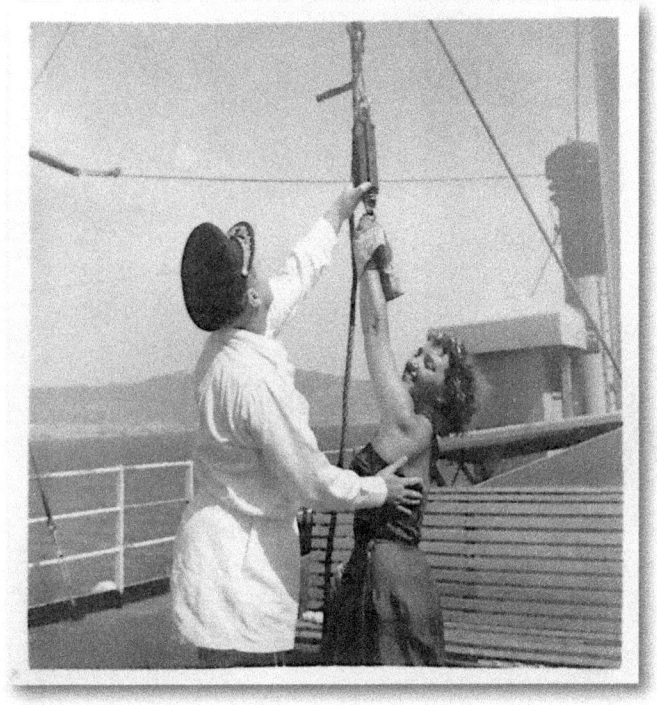

"Crew Assistant" Kate Salter

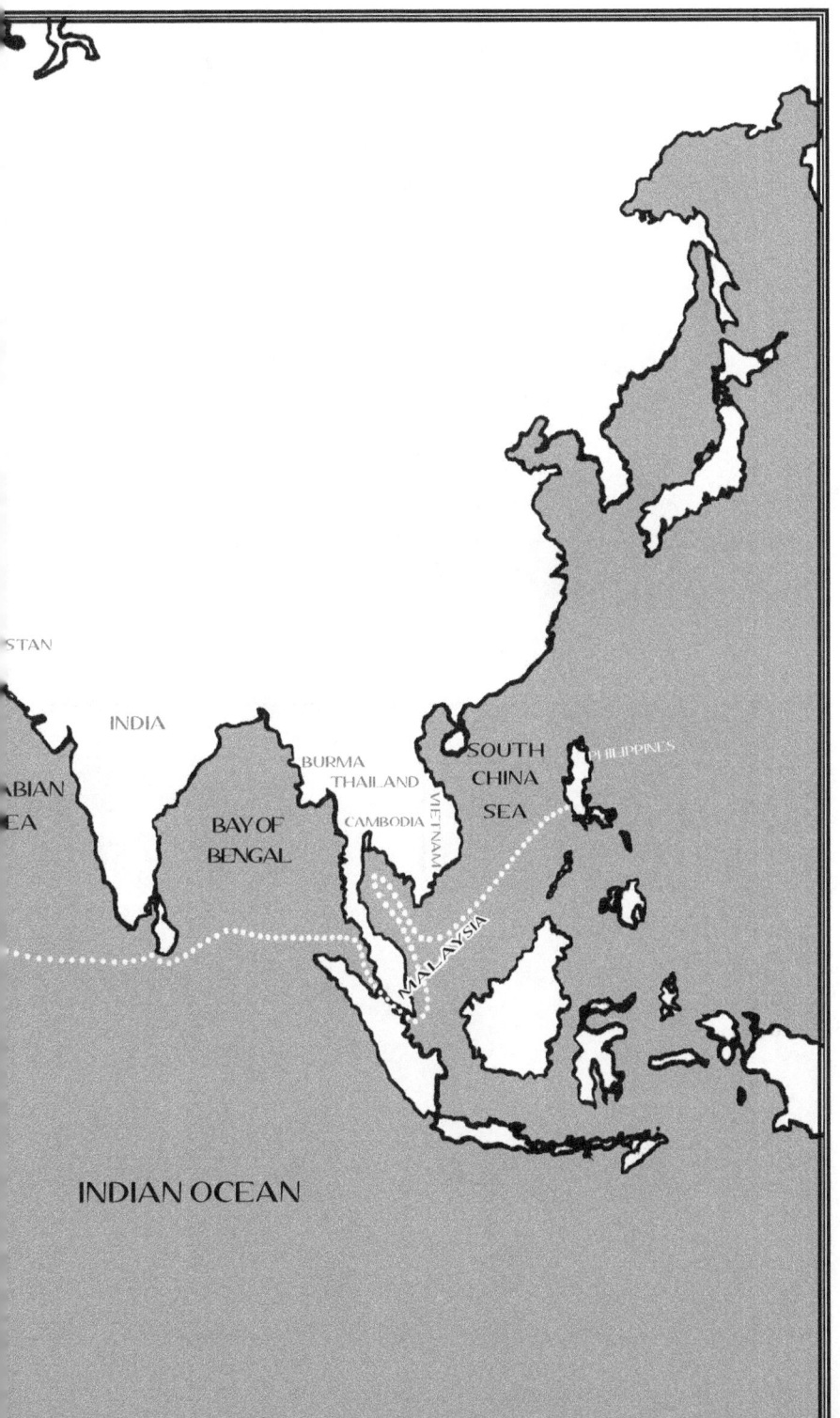

East Asiatic Line Brochures

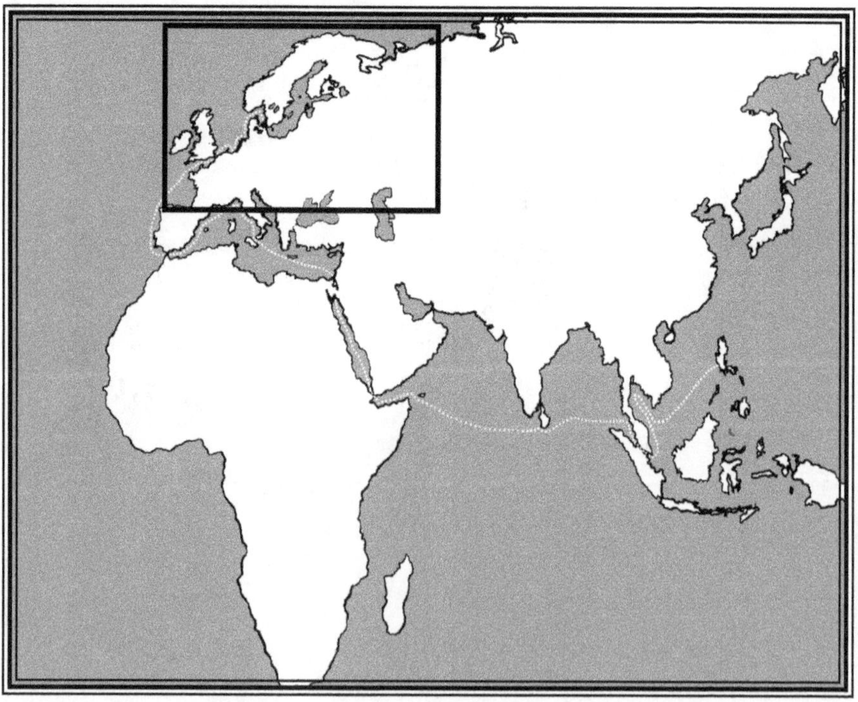

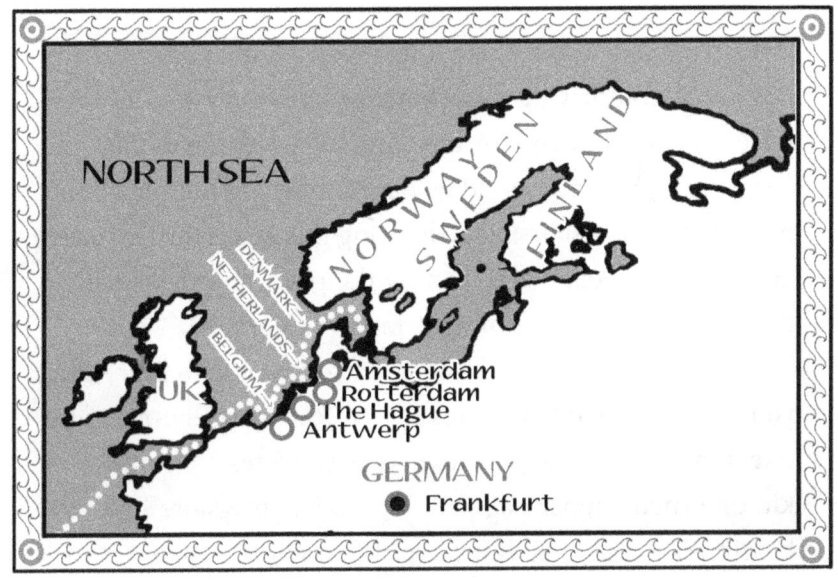

Can This Be Me in Cabin G?

December 1949

Well, my darlings, this is it! The first page of what may turn out to be the most exciting thing I ever do—my journey around the world on board the MS *Mongolia*. I feel so tremulously "on the brink" that I am tongue-tied before my beloved typewriter and my mental images of each of your faces. If I write too much it is because this is not really a letter but rather a complete journal of my adventures. I am trying to make seven carbon copies, so I hope you find your copy legible.

To begin, I should describe this little spot from which I am writing. You have undoubtedly heard of a bedroom made over into a bathroom. Well, I think I am in a bathroom made into a bedroom. It is tiny, with tiled walls and a cement floor, tucked under the eaves of a very obscure Dutch hotel in a far corner of

Rotterdam. After piling into a taxi with *all* my possessions in the world and driving from hotel to hotel only to find there were no rooms to rent in this city, I was overjoyed that this "pension" type place would take me in. It is up four incredibly narrow flights of stairs; its redeeming graces are the two eager and friendly people who manage the place and the small gas heater, which is blazing away at my feet right now.

Though it is one hell of a bother to travel with everything you own lying in odd bundles at your feet—namely, one radio, one typewriter, one briefcase, two suitcases, one make-up kit, one small zipper bag with a portable drugstore in it, one bulging B-4 bag, two duffel bags of which one does not lock at all, and the other, though securely locked at the top, has a wide gap at the bottom, and finally an invaluable camera bag which weighs more than I do and has to be carried wherever I go, plus my maps of the world—this sentence is too long to finish! The gist of it is that once in a small room, out comes my spare pillows and pink eiderdown, my cognac flask, my small library, my perfume and creams, my flannel nightgown, my tripod camera, my typewriter and carbons…on goes my radio and life is ready to be lived in comfort!

You should have seen the wide-eyed amazement of the Dutch hotel owner who popped into my room with a tray of cheese, bread and tea. She took one look around this little closet which I have made so cheery and cozy and asked if she could bring her ten year old son up to see my radio. Benevolently, I agreed and have been showing off my belongings for the past half hour. In so doing I have discovered that my two French records need go no farther on this globe-circling junket, for they are already broken. Always quick to rationalize, I consider it lucky that it happened on the first day of the trip and not the last.

I had a delicious goose dinner with Palmer last night at the British Club in Frankfurt. We toasted each other up and down, and she got a kick out of telling two Englishmen whom we met that, "You'll have to excuse us, for Miss Salter is going to the Philippines now!"

Can this be me? I still cannot believe it. Yesterday, when I awoke and sleepily curled up under my beloved quilt and said deliberately to myself, "Today I go around the world on a freighter." I just could not grasp that it was anything but a joke. I remember a similar experience when I was eight and I awoke and said, "Today, summer vacation begins," and I would say it over and over again because it was too good to be true, and yet it was true.

My train departed Frankfurt at about one in the morning, which is an ungodly hour for people to be up and about seeing trains off, but my favorite office people were there. They practically came on the trip with me because these European trains start up with absolutely no warning, and there they all were—in the middle of the train—when suddenly we became aware that the train was pulling out of the Frankfurt station.

My trip started off with a definite bang when a longhaired, arrogant porter raised absolute hell when he saw the endless stream of luggage which was being whisked from the platform into my compartment. I had purchased a private compartment, for I was afraid of customs trouble with my camera equipment and I wanted to cope with it with a maximum of privacy and skill.

Fortunately, a charming English friend of Martha helped the station porter get the luggage into the train so that I didn't need the help of the obnoxious train porter. But as soon as the train left Frankfurt, the porter approached me with a livid face, screaming at me in German that this was not a baggage car and that my luggage would have to go to the baggage car, and that furthermore, I'd have to pay ten pounds extra, etcetera, etcetera, etcetera! He began to get the better of me until finally I got so mad that I started stomping up and down the train demanding that I speak to his superior. This fellow had the nerve to tell me he would not make up my bed because there wasn't room for him to do so. This was the final straw. After all, I had a first-class ticket just so my baggage would not be a bother to anyone else. I started to rip my compartment apart myself, and the more imperious I became, the more I enjoyed it. Who was this mad woman who was giving a porter hell on the Orient Express? Can you believe it was me? It ended with me the victor—tucked into a cozy bunk, going sound asleep with my worldly goods contentedly sharing my first class room and not banished to the baggage car after all.

Customs was tense because by law I should have had to pay duty for my Leica and Rolleiflex. The German officials understood that I had arrived that day at Rhein-Main Air Base and hadn't had time to buy anything in Germany, so they did not investigate. Once the train was on its way, it was then up to the Dutch officials who probed about but let all my possessions go through duty-free.

I even took a picture today though it was freezing cold and very stormy. I made myself go out in spite of the weather. The sun finally came out as I was standing on the waterfront.

A woman popped out to the deck of her canal boat and started doing her wash in a washing machine built right on deck. A perfect picture, but I was embarrassed to take it. Since my whole body was aching from carrying my photographic equipment around, the fact that a fine picture presented itself to me and I was too timid to take it seemed the final straw. So I gave myself a stern little lecture, parked my equipment on a pile of junk on the wharf, and calmly and deliberately took the picture. Now I am a foreign correspondent!

This letter is far too detailed, but I am writing the details to enhance my memory when it is over. My ship has been delayed another day because of the stormy weather, so tomorrow I will go to Antwerp. I love you all, and being able to write you about my journey as I go will enhance the wonder of the trip one hundredfold. It already has!

Aboard the MS *Mongolia* in Antwerp

After the crushing news that my ship would be a day late, I prepared to sightsee around Rotterdam, but not with much enthusiasm, for it is a cold, rainy December day. My hotel keeper suggested I go to The Hague and I was flabbergasted to discover that it was only twenty minutes away. I went to a museum which had seven of the most beautiful Rembrandts I ever hope to see, as well as three or four exceptional Vermeers. The two best paintings in the collection were Rembrandt's painting of the physicians and Vermeer's divine "Lady in the Blue Hat." After a fancy lunch in The Hague, I returned to Rotterdam only to learn that the *Mongolia* would be still a day later.

Having waited a lifetime for this day, I felt I couldn't stand it another minute, so I checked on trains to Antwerp. The tinyness of Europe never ceases to amaze me; I found that I was only two hours from Antwerp. So I stored my luggage and—armed with typewriter, radio and camera, the weight of which is agonizingly piercing on my shoulder—I "entrained" for Antwerp. In the excitement and rigmarole of customs (six officials between the borders), I went right past Antwerp and found myself speeding towards Brussels with no way to "detrain." I had to pay extra fare both ways, had no Belgian currency, and added extra hours to my unexpected arrival at the *Mongolia*. By the time I was on a train back to Antwerp, I had that cold, lonely, broke, lost, and helpless feeling that I abhor. (It's funny how many possible emotions we carry around with us each day, some of which we never use. It is months and months since I have felt that way, and it is a terrifying and very revealing experience.) I boarded a taxi at the station and asked the driver to try to locate the *Mongolia*. We drove around the glistening wet waterfront, past looming hulks of ships, to the doorways of several locked customs houses and pilots' quarters, and finally found her. She lay in the center of a hectic loading area, which was teeming with activity in spite of the fact that it was now midnight. Loud cries protested the arrival of the taxi to this forbidden area. They changed to sudden silence as the American girl stepped out into the rain with her bundles and announced that she would be boarding the ship. I paid the taxi driver so that there could be no retreat and went on board. A young boy with curly hair and a navy cap on the back of his head who so reminds me of my brother, Joel, took over with great delight and dashed off to find the Chief Steward after I announced that I was Miss Salter. I climbed under a rope leading to the gangplank and in a few short steps I was aboard! I could hardly contain my trembling as the steward unlocked Cabin G.

Cabin G! It is a dream! It is about seven by nine feet. It is shining and white, has a desk-dresser, a washbasin, a closet, a radiator, an electric fan, a very comfortable ship's bed, a big porthole, and lamps in almost every corner of the room. It is next door to a big and beautifully equipped bathroom. Once I get back to Rotterdam to get my eiderdown and maps for the wall, my cosmetics, cotton blouses and perfume, etcetera, I will never want to leave this little cubbyhole. The stewards and waiters and cooks whom I have seen look remarkably handsome and friendly. Until tomorrow, I am the only passenger on board, and after that I will still be the only American. After three years of living with Americans in Europe, it is going to be a great, great experience to be the only one in sight for the next six and a half weeks.

I really couldn't sleep when I finally did go to bed because of the racket the cranes made outside my window, and the knowledge that I was at last on my ship of ships. I also was kept awake by the voices of the dockhands and the expectation of daylight when I could really see what this whole ship looked like.

A handsome young Dane popped his head in to wake me at eight o'clock and I had breakfast in lonely splendor…bacon and eggs, coffee and rolls. I strolled around the deck during the morning taking pictures as the crew loaded the hold with huge wicker baskets marked "Hong Kong," and sacks of something or other marked "Bangkok," and huge kegs of German beer marked "Manila." I walked through the airy, carpeted passageways which are reserved for the twelve passengers. There are six rooms on either side of the ship and the dining room is at one end. At the other end there is a small, plush lounge equipped with card tables, radio, Victrola, couches, and some comfortable chairs. If I had a million dollars, I wouldn't want to take this trip on any other sort of vessel. Twelve is the perfect number, and the significance of carrying cargo instead of just prattling American tourists makes it all a thousand times more real and vital and worthwhile.

I think lunch was my biggest surprise. The Captain, Chief Mate, his wife, who returns to Denmark tomorrow, and I had a table to ourselves. On this table were twenty serving bowls of chicken, fish, potatoes, cheese, ham salad, herring, sardines, shrimp, rolls, and delicacies which I couldn't begin to recognize. As the meal progressed, there were five clean plates set before me and in the background a constant battery of young waiters looking to my every want. It was like a Henry the Eighth movie with Kate in the role of Henry—only with better manners. The same Kate probably did not have more than ten regular meals during these last two months in Europe. As a beverage I had a cold glass of Danish beer, which is strong and perfect with such things as raw, salted herring and shimmery little sardines eaten with gusto. After crackers, cheese, and fruit, we retired to the lounge for coffee. I am sure that I sat there grinning from ear to ear and pinching myself to make sure this was real. The Captain assured me that this is the regular luncheon and that I can count on such banquets for the next six weeks. I'm going to love eating again!

The Captain just asked if I was going ashore as we got up from our luncheon demitasse in the lounge. "No, I don't think so," I replied. "I've spent my life ashore." And I popped away to try to settle myself focusing on my typewriter.

I feel as though I just disproved the age-old saying that if you look forward to something too much you will spoil it. I find that the *Mongolia* exceeds my wildest dreams, and by now I even like its name.

This trip has the makings of paradise, because it combines travel with the snug security of having your own little nest and people who will be friendly and watch out for you, and yet who have no jurisdiction over you. I am settling down with a sigh of contentment and come what may, when I meet up with my father in Manila, this trip will be worth any price.

8 December 1949—Slipping into the North Sea from Antwerp

If there is such a thing as a honeymoon for one, then I am on it. We are sailing—this huge, lovely, gleaming white ship with its Danish crew, its cargo of mysterious bundles for the Far East, its fog horns and sirens, its immaculate stewards, its gruff old Captain, its pilot to guide us into Rotterdam, and *I* the only passenger! After forty women to a compartment on my last trans-Atlantic voyage from the U.S. to Germany, it is beyond my wildest dreams to have a complete and perfect ship all to myself. The stewards are very attentive. My bath is drawn, my second cup of tea poured, my every need attended to with such speed that I hardly know the project is started. I just noticed that a rug and new bedspread have been added to my stateroom within the last five minutes. It is like being a queen! Never have I felt such luxurious contentment.

Yesterday afternoon the Dutch pilot for Rotterdam boarded the ship. The steward invited me to join him for cake and strong black Danish coffee. Since we were not to sail until after midnight, he took me ashore to see Antwerp and we had a marvelous time. I have just been reading Mark Twain's *Life on the Mississippi*, and this made talking to a real sea pilot an awesome experience. This man delighted in telling me about Holland and about experiences he has had piloting ships. I was an eager listener when I wasn't being an eager talker. I think one of his funniest accounts was comparing an American seaman, which he pronounced "sheeman" with his Dutch or Scandinavian counterpart. He said a Captain of a European ship is very formal with the pilot, but at the same time never leaves his side at the bridge during tight spots or when the pilot is getting accustomed to a new ship. An American Captain, however, comes up to the pilot, slaps him on the back, calls him "Captain" in a familiar manner, shakes his hand warmly, turns the ship over to him, and then retires to his bunk below, letting the pilot get along as best he can up on the bridge.

Two funny things happened yesterday. First is that I had the awful thought that perhaps the meals were not included in the price of the trip. I finally got up the courage to ask the Captain. He assured me that they were included and was surprised to find out I hadn't been informed of that fact. The second thing was when a very determined and pompous young Belgian immigration official came on board to "immigrate" me. He asked bossily why I was going to Manila and I suddenly realized that I didn't know. I could have told him about dreams of trips around the world, or freelance writing, or the lure of places unknown but I just told him: "Because I want to." He thought that was the most idiotic statement ever given an immigration official. Ah the joy of being a "crazy American" as they call us.

9 December 1949—At the Dockside in Rotterdam

It is evening now and I've finished my after-dinner coffee and retired to my stateroom. I've donned my frilly new housecoat, contemplated my flask of cognac and box of chocolates, smiled happily to myself in the mirror, and am now settling in with my typewriter.

We pulled into the Rotterdam quay yesterday afternoon and it was a wet, bedraggled cluster of Englishwomen who herded aboard. So far we have two Englishwomen with one child each who are going to Malaya and Borneo to join their husbands. Also, there is one Carrie Hall-type of English woman who has been everywhere and done everything, and has a story to fill every pause, and is joining her husband in Singapore, and another mousy, quiet wife and her humorous banker husband (also English) who are bound for Japan. In Marseille, we get two more children and their parents or parent, and in Genoa we gain a Japanese-German woman. It is not going to be what you would call a "grand romance" sort of trip, but the romance I have longed for and want the most is definitely here—and that is with Kate and this ship and the sea.

It is truly a dream ship. The smallness is perfect and yet it looks huge as I stand back on the dock and try to take artistic pictures of it. The stewards and waiters are wonderfully attentive, not in the obsequious manner of the Germans, but in a sort of friendly rapport as though they have been waiting for their entire career for such a one as you to be a passenger. Starting tomorrow morning, they are going to bring me tea in bed so that getting up will be even more luxurious than it already is.

The meals continue to be twenty meals in one. The poor English folk aboard are beside themselves with ecstasy over such bounty. They have been eating rations lower than the Germans and suddenly a year's worth of rations appears on the table at one meal. We still haven't introduced ourselves and I am not going to be the eager American who goes about calling them by their first names, as I'm sure they are secretly anticipating.

I laughed when I saw the luggage in front of the banker's stateroom. There was a set of golf clubs, a bundle of guns, and a large wicker hamper. I can just see the cold fowl and white wine being tucked away by his cook already!

I suppose I sin by talking about where I have been too much, for it is such a fascinating subject to oneself. But the more I hear soft British accents murmuring over Calcutta, Baghdad, Singapore, Burma, and Hong Kong, the more I vow never to even let it be known that I have taken the 7th Avenue Subway from Yonkers to downtown Manhattan. It is a deadly bore to have some new continent, territory, province, city, or island pulled from thin air to prove a point when no geography is needed at all for the discussion. It always gives me a nervous feeling as though I, too, should get to Malaya before I can count myself a truly traveled person. After each meal I dash to my room and get out my map so as to discover where all these places are. The casual reference to coolies as servants, "sahib" ports and planes and ships and motoring is certainly a far cry from American conversation and it is quite fun for a while. I've been the laughed-at American for so long, it's fun to laugh at the Brits for a change. The most amazing moment was when the British complained of the horrors of central heating. After my one weekend in the English countryside with Barbara and Charles, dressed in long underwear, scarf and coat, indoors, I simply find it hard to believe that anyone from that land of chills could object to a furnace. Also, American cooking…but, we do agree on this Danish cooking, and I expect I shall gain a stone before this trip is over.

Today, I had a marvelous time taking pictures. I feel a bit hypocritical passing myself off as a photographer, but one look at my Leica slung carelessly over my shoulder convinces any bystander that I am the real McCoy, and I get one-hundred percent cooperation. The trouble I have is focusing. By the time the Leica is in gear, so to speak, my subject has dropped his pile of hay, jug of acid, barrel of beer, or whatever it is he is putting in the hold, and stands grinning at me. I try to tell him to "work" in every language I know but this just brings out wider smiles and forced stances for the picture. Some of the moments were rather dangerous because the workers were so intent on getting their picture taken that they paid no attention to the hundreds of pounds of goods swaying off cranes perilously close to them. A few of the ship's officers came up with the intention of telling me that I was in forbidden territory, but when I snapped a picture of them they rather sheepishly wandered on, leaving me reigning supreme with the workmen. Before this trip is over, I plan to wedge into every corner of the ship and really get some pictures. I am going to make a wonderful scrapbook and bring my children up on it.

You should see my boudoir now. My pink quilt is fluffed out on my bunk, my extra pillows are at the head of my bed, my darling doll is resting on a pillow; I have a big map and book on a small bedside table; I have a huge bouquet of flowers on my dresser, compliments of the East Asiatic Company, along with an entire counter of creams, powders, perfumes, soap, lipstick, and finally my wonderful Chamberlain calendar. Anyway, everything I need is tucked away in this tiny, luxurious stateroom—even Scotch tape!

There is a routine of leisure, regular mealtime and teatime, comfortable sleeping, and time for writing and reading. All this is founded on a thrill of excitement because of the harbor, the glorious noises of the steamers going past us, the whistles and cries and sirens and bells and sea gull noises, and the sense of expectancy mixed with permanency, which is the perfect combination. You can have all of the adventure in the world without the scare of dark alleyways, no room to be had in a hotel, expensive taxis, no one to talk to, or too much insecurity which accompany many a new adventure. Maybe at the end of six weeks I'll be glad to leave the *Mongolia*, but at the moment, I think I could gladly live on a ship for the rest of time.

One thing I enjoy: I am the only woman who is going somewhere because *she* is the motivating factor. Everyone else is a wife joining a husband, and though I envy them their husbands, at the same time I adore being independent and purposeful and self-activating. I sense that my diamond earrings, two cameras, suede jacket, a different ensemble every day, and high heels are regarded as "rich American" by the others. This might be my imagination, but the point is that it is such fun to look at all of my lovely belongings and think of the happiness I have on this beautiful ship and know that I earned every penny of this myself.

MS *Mongolia*

A needed rest.

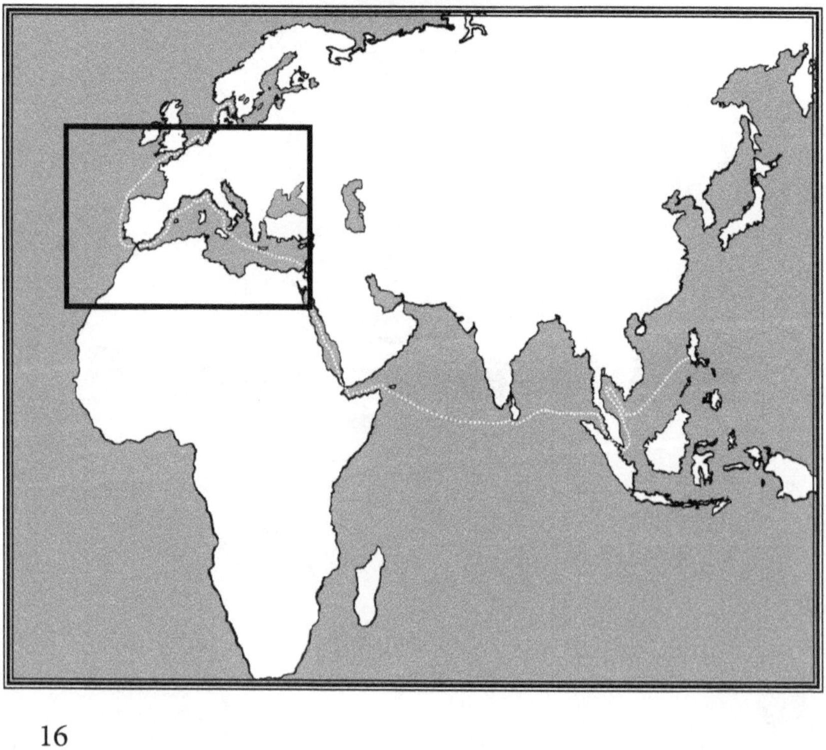

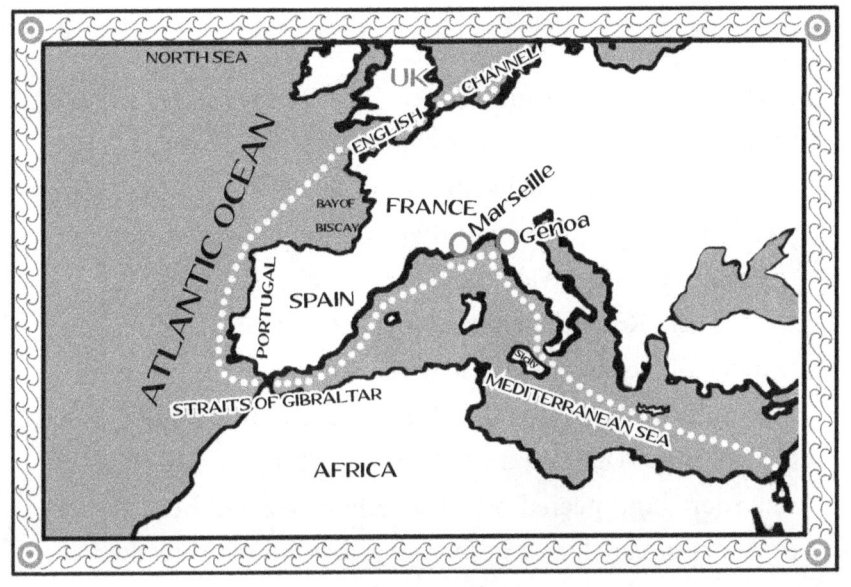

The Blue, Blue Mediterranean

11 December 1949—Bay of Biscay

The English Channel chapter of this journal is doomed never to be written, at least not while actually on the English Channel, for Miss Salter was definitely indisposed and lying on her bed of pain in a frothy blue ensemble with stewards dashing about with tea and crackers and sympathetic glances.

I don't even mind being seasick on this trip. Everything is so utterly perfect that an unsettled stomach is a small ailment beside so much bliss. Anyway, compared to the strictness of Army transports—where you were not supposed to be lying in your bunk between nine and eleven because of inspection, and under no circumstances could you have any food brought to your bunk—not to mention the fact that there were thirty or forty other people wailing around below you, above you, and next to you—this business of retiring to a delectable chamber, tumbling beneath a silky eiderdown, having stewards come in of their own initiative, having them beg you to let them bring you something, and then having a fellow passenger drop in to see if she can help. Well, it just makes being sick a pleasure.

We left Rotterdam the night of the ninth, and it was a wonderful departure. I had been typing in my room and was almost ready for bed, when I heard unmistakable noises of departure. I put on a coat, dashed to the deck next to my stateroom, and peered over the railing. We had been docked in a sort of canal, and in front and behind us were shadowy vessels from England, Holland and Sweden. Up and down the canal and into the open stretch of water just ahead of us were small black tugs chugging away with sparkling red and green lights and clouds of smoke coming from their stacks and the insistent jangle of signaling bells and sirens. A large moon with a tiny scarf of a cloud was shining down on our canal and shining back again from the water. Lights from the quay, the other boats, and our own ship were reflected all along the canal, and the indistinct figures of sailors, dock workers, and tug boat captains moved about in the darkness calling out to one another in Danish and in Dutch. It was a thrilling moment. Three tugs puffed and fumed away at our port side, jostling for the right position to pull our twelve thousand-ton ship out into the main stream. Finally, with a lot of whistle signaling going back and forth and the huge roar of our steamer horn, the *Mongolia* was slowly pulled away from the quay and we headed for the Orient!

I stood bundled in my warm red coat with my scarf around

my neck and laughed to myself as I remembered the woman in Madison, Wisconsin who sold me the coat and told me it would be perfect for going to football games. Football games!... and going to the Orient, I might add. I hurried back to my room and hopped into bed, pulling my beautiful quilt up around me and trying to realize that the gentle swaying of the ship meant that I was at last on my way.

Yesterday was quite interesting, for bit by bit we are beginning to know one another. I imagine that eventually this journal will be quite full of accounts of the passengers. Now I will give my first impressions. Hopefully this won't be dreadfully boring, but when I'm rereading this journal in my dotage it will bring back all the memories.

There is one passenger about whom her "acquaintances" (and I use that word advisedly) must have said to themselves, "Boy! I certainly feel sorry for the passengers stranded on a freighter with *her* for six weeks." She talks *all* the time. She listens to no one, except to the extent to hear when they pause for breath so that she can chime in with accounts of her cousins, her husband, her mother-in-law, or her last trip to the East, ad nauseam, and then some. She makes me look into myself for I am afraid I have some of those same tendencies, and by the time this trip is over I think I'll know better. How it stifles conversation, for no one can ever get any theme started without having this stocky little woman jump in and swamp the whole thing. She and I have been having a few American-English conflicts, which are making me realize what a patriot I am, and how I wouldn't want to be any other nationality for anything on earth. This particular woman's name is Mrs. Peter Warren (for future reference), and she is bound for

19

Batavia to see her contractor husband. She is the rather lumpy kind of woman who does not look well in clothes and so she says she considers them unimportant and glares at you when you arrive for dinner in a shapely little costume, which makes clothing seem delightful.

There is another woman, Gabriel O'Neil, who has coined the perfect name (Mrs. W.) for the lumpy Englishwoman. She and her six-year-old daughter, Sheila, are joining Sean O'Neil who is employed by the Malayan government to put down uprisings among the natives. Gabriel—who I soon began calling "Gay"—has gone out of her way to be gracious and charming, and though we are just getting acquainted I feel that she and I may grow to be very good friends. She came in last night to inquire about how I felt since I had not come to dinner. She stayed to tell me that in the Orient there simply are no single women and that I would be wined and dined and proposed to until I was dizzy. As you know, I am not counting on social life to make my stay in Manila fun, but it is a wonderful thing to have someone volunteer this kind of information and to look at you with sparkling eyes and envy your adventures-to-come! She has already invited me to visit her in Singapore any time I want to. I might add that all four women aboard seem to be about the same age, between twenty-seven and thirty-two.

There is a third Englishwoman with a six-year-old daughter. She is very thin, really very nice, and has just given up a secretarial job in order to join her husband in Borneo. Apparently, she has never been out of England before, and she is both scared and thrilled at what lies ahead, but also a little sorrowful about leaving a good job behind. I imagine she will be nice rather than interesting.

But the people who have contributed the most so far are the banker and his wife. The wife is a tiny blonde with straightish hair, too much rouge, and does not say a word. This quality is becoming increasingly a virtue as I hear Mrs. W. ramble on incessantly. The banker is a large man with horn-rimmed spectacles, and already is appearing in grey flannels, ascot tie, tweed coat, and pipe. He has a very contagious smile and the gift of making anything he says interesting. Apparently his wife is Canadian—their name is Price by the way—and she was teaching in a private school in China when the war broke out. She and the entire school were put in a concentration camp and held there for nearly four years. Mr. Price was put into the same camp, and there they met, fell in love, became engaged and were married. To hear his accounts of the camp is a priceless experience.

He apparently was made the master baker and stood in dough up to his neck, patting loaves and watching yeast rise. To hear a very proper Englishman dressed in his tweeds describe what is involved in being a master baker for fourteen hundred people is quite an experience. I am looking forward very much to learning about Ruth Price's adventures as a school teacher in the Orient, for that is something I am definitely considering when I run out of money. If I can ever get her away from Mrs. W., I'll have a chance to ask some questions, but in a group that is impossible, as Mrs. W. has enough school teacher stories to consume twenty-four hours worth of conversation, and by then we've all gone to sleep.

All of these Englishfolk are conservatives and just waiting for the day their government will change. According to Mr. Price, you can get free false teeth and four pairs of free glasses but no food, under the present regime. I adore hearing them talk about politics. One funny thing I forgot to mention is that Mr. Price said when the Americans liberated their concentration camp, they parachuted pounds of Chiclets to the prisoners! I love the Americans!

12 December 1949—Atlantic Ocean, off the Coast of Spain

It is an incredibly beautiful day with a fresh breeze, sun, deep blue ocean, and a feeling of ease and optimism over us all. I think we are turning into quite a happy and friendly group, and the entire atmosphere is definitely homelike and civilized. After this past year in the Occupation where one was almost never invited into a living room or for a home-cooked meal, it is heaven to sit around a fireplace and have a cup of after-dinner coffee and pleasant conversation. The excellence of the cuisine continues and I am already gaining weight, looking better and feeling better. Each afternoon I nap after lunch until tea-time. I'll be glad when the sunbathing weather is here. I feel a bit decadent. One push of the bell delivers morning tea. Another push and my evening bath is drawn. One of the greatest delights continues to be roaming around the ship with my Leica that seems to be a passport to forbidden places.

I think I have my sea legs now, and my stomach is well on the mend. I have ordered a deck chair and spend as much of my spare time tucked beneath my eiderdown overlooking the sea.

One thing that continues to amaze me about the English is the fact that they hardly know anything about Europe. I am the only passenger who has traveled on "the continent," as they say. They are far more conversant with the ways of Eastern natives than those of the French, Italians, and Germans who live next door.

I brought a hush to the conversation last night when the group was speaking of the joys of native servants from the hills of places like Borneo, Malaya or Iraq, and the shattering catastrophe of being forced to hire from the cities, for such servants were so "dreadfully spoiled." I had been hearing about this sad plight for several days and was feeling no sympathy. So last night I said, "Just what do you mean by spoiled? It seems to me that the way you use the word brings up a question of definition." There was a stunned silence as they mentally made note of these "upstart Americans and their talk of independence" and finally Mrs. W. (to be sure!) launched into a detailed account of how "sahib's" socks were stolen, and by then it was my bedtime.

Mrs. W. and I were left at the tea table yesterday and we had quite a talk, which makes me a bit more sympathetic towards her endless domination of the conversational scene in spite of everybody's unspoken protest. She has Hodgkin's disease, and ten years ago was given just six months to live. She seems to have carried on in spite of it all, but expects to die at any moment, perhaps. It is hard to know what to say to someone whom you do not know at all who tells you this, and I did quite a bit of mental scurrying around for the proper response. She credits her long survival with being desperately in love with the man to whom she is married. This is one unusual thing I have observed in our group. Everyone is married and seems to be deeply in love with his or her mate—without any doubts or questioning. Is that more of an English characteristic than American?

The cold weather is definitely over, and I often dash up to my favorite unsheltered spot on the upper deck with only a sweater as a wrap. There I stand with spray dashing against my face and that glorious, tangy, salty air blowing me almost out to sea. I feel unbridled happiness as I realize that it is Kate and she is on the Bay of Biscay bound for Gibraltar, the Indian Ocean, and Bangkok. It is something that I still cannot fully realize, although bit by bit a heavenly sense of leisure and fulfilled expectation is creeping into me. I suppose one of the things most responsible for my current sense of well-being is the wonderful food—quite a change from the meager rations I was eating in Germany.

I seem to have become the favored passenger who sits on the Captain's right at all meals when he is at our table. The others have been jostled around a little, but I am always in the spot of honor. What fun. The ship's officers look just the way Danish sailing men should look. The First Mate looks like Jean Gabin and is very dashing in a deeply rugged way. The Captain is rather old, weather-beaten, very stern, extremely gallant, most dapper in his uniform, and quite amused that I am a "journalist." He has promised to let me up on the forbidden bridge to get a picture of him in action.

We have one "stowaway..." a black cat who strolled on board in Rotterdam and spends his time proudly stalking around the poop deck and sharpening his claws on neatly coiled ropes which lie all over the lower decks. That is what I call one adventuresome cat—to walk up a gangplank and take a trip to the Orient all on its own initiative!

13 December 1949—Straits of Gibraltar—at the Rock of Gibraltar

A most startling development came up at dinner last night. One of the passengers asked the First Mate why they were fixing up the aft hold and he replied, "I guess we'd better by the time we come to Genoa. After all, we have a princess aboard!" We all looked a bit nervously towards the aft hold and sure enough, the Mate confirmed our worst fear. An Italian princess or, more precisely, an Italian duchess, was riding in state down there in a coffin. She was being returned to Genoa for an Italian funeral. This, coupled with the black cat on board and the ship's departure on Friday the thirteenth, are three ominous portents, which as yet have not been fulfilled.

Two nights ago at twilight we passed a most beautiful ship. It was low, long, and graceful, with a small center part of white which rose high from the sea amid many lights, and the rest of the ship was black and sleek. She looked like a gentleman freighter. As I watched this phantom ship pass in the night and wondered whether we looked half as beautiful, our ship called out a signal of greeting with its rumbling horn, and the other ship promptly answered. At dinner I was told that this was our sister ship, the MS *Morelia*, bound for Denmark from Australia.

14 December 1949

The Mediterranean Sea with the shoreline of Spain is a matter of minutes away. As I glance to my right from this desk in my stateroom, I see a green swell, sharp brown cliffs which come right down to the white surf below, and a shade of brilliant light blue with heavy silvery clouds scattered about it. It is beautiful and exciting, for those cliffs are the cliffs of Spain and they are almost within swimming distance from me. On our ship radio we hear nothing but Spanish tangos, and there is nothing like a Spanish tango coming right from tango country!

Yesterday there were some very beautiful moments too, for on one side of the ship lay Africa and on the other lay Spain. Mr. Price, the banker, called out excitedly in a very British accent, "I say, there's Gib! There she is all right. Old Gib!" And that was the Rock of Gibraltar which rises stark and barren from the sea, with a backdrop of snow-capped mountains, a tiny red-roofed Spanish village on the distant shoreline behind it, and all of the glamour of countless geography lessons making it a most momentous thing to see. I took a million pictures of it from all angles and am only sorry that someone couldn't take my picture as I was looking at it. I did get a shot of a very young Danish sailor taking a picture of it with his box camera.

And speaking of cameras and the like, I find myself in a rather unusual position for a Salter. I seem to be too rich. Can you imagine such a thing! I feel the way I used to feel when I wore Pat's diamond watch in the subway. My colorful clothes, my eiderdown, my typewriter, my Leica and then my Rolleiflex, and my dollar currency, all cause the British to look at me rather aloofly (a combination of jealousy and disdain), and I feel as though I should explain that I have no money in the bank, and that I really don't have so many clothes but oft mix my skirts and blouses around, and that the Leica and the Rolleiflex are my ticket to America. I am almost afraid of the time I shall bring my portable radio on deck. I think I will be ostracized. I find I am better at carrying off the role of a pauper than a princess.

16 December 1949—Dockside in Marseille

This will have to be speedy, for we leave within an hour and the wind is so overpowering on deck that I can barely stand. What it will be like once we are out of this protected harbor I shudder to think. I can see that until our arrival at six tomorrow morning in Genoa I shall be prostrate on my bunk…oh, well!…the life of a sailor!

I've just come back from a most invigorating jaunt into Marseille. I've been to the city several times before, always under a cloud of misery and depression and hopelessness. The heaven it has been to go up to the Old Harbor and wander around in the bright sunlight with my present frame of mind is something glorious. The contrast is like day and night. It is what you call a "bracing day" and all of the fishwives, excursion boats, and oystermen were going strong in the city. I seem to have pulled some photographic courage out of nowhere, for I walk right up under the noses of these people, deliberately focus my camera, and snap a picture. Only a few months ago I would see a good picture but never dare to take it. It is wonderful what a little courage will accomplish.

I also was able to cash in on my dearest love—Yardley's. It is terribly cheap here, and I bought soap, lavender water, and hand cream. I just adore the fresh, lovely smell. I would have bought quantities more, but the English women aboard seem to find themselves in the position of having pounds but no one wants them, and I am the only person with negotiable cash. Quite a novel predicament for me.

The ship *Mongolia* arrived in Marseille last night after dark, and it was a breathtaking sight to see a glimmer of light on the horizon and then gradually approach a fairyland of harbor lights, sparkling jewels which were scattered all over the inland blackness of the shore. The most fun was to see the French pilot come aboard. (There goes the steamer horn!—we are pulling out.)

I told you about the proud "Jean Gabin" type of man who sort of stalked aboard as we entered the North Sea. In France it was quite a different thing. I saw a tiny green and red light in the distance which I took for a buoy, but as it seemed suddenly to be charging upon us I realized it must be a small boat. The waves were really pretty terrific, and when the little tug finally got near to the rope ladder, it would rise up for nearly twelve feet or more and then suddenly sink down twelve feet. Out of the tiny door of the cabin popped a dynamic little fellow, done up in a fur trimmed trench coat and a natty blue beret. Like a jack-in-the-box he shot up the rope ladder before any normal person would ever have discovered its location! He was agile to the nth degree. It was fun to see something so typically French—even in a harbor pilot, which I should think would have a nationality all its own.

An awfully nice thing happened as I was writing. Mrs. O'Neil just came to my door with a handful of adorable ceramic earrings and asked me to take my pick. I had bought a small doll for her daughter when I was on shore, for the little girl is sick, and they were so grateful that she felt she had to give me a present. After the barren emotional ground of Germany, I find myself extremely susceptible to anything which is a warm acceptance. I shouldn't generalize, but if any such thing as warm acceptance existed in the Occupation, it only was in a very few people.

One wonderful thing about the *Mongolia* is the fact that since it is so heavily weighted with cargo, we have a ten times smoother sailing than we would in a passenger ship of the same size. Our cargo is amazing. I still know only tidbits of it but I am making a list of questions to ask "Jean Gabin," the First Mate. In addition to the corpse of the princess, there is frozen pheasant, lily-of-the-valley seeds, and sulphuric acid.

I bought some Nivea sun cream today, but some of the more seasoned travelers think I may not even need it. I shall be absolutely crushed if I'm not a rich shade of olive brown by the time I reach the dock in Manila.

I've been having my fortune told by cards and palmistry and there are all sorts of revealing things being said, such as "a fair, older man who will become a terribly good friend,"—"A plan which will be dashed to the ground and not go through, but a dark man who will arrive to make everything all right,"—"a legacy from a remote cousin or friend who will soon die in the night"—and "an engagement which was suddenly broken to be followed by a marriage which is controlled more by the head than the heart." I find myself waiting with bated breath for each new prophecy and shuddering at the "change of plan" and thrilling to "the dark-haired man who is to be such a good friend." Wait till I come home, and I'll put on my best gypsy earrings and really give each of you a plunge into black magic!

I've discovered one strange characteristic in the English. No one ever really gives compliments. I think they consider it rude to do so. Mrs. O'Neil will look with gasping delight at some lovely embroidered blouse of mine, but will say nothing. Then when her daughter, Sheila, comes up to me and says, "My, Auntie, you look lovely!" (for some reason she calls me Auntie, which gives me the heebie-jeebies), I take her into the corner and tell her to call me Kate. Apparently her mother takes her into another corner and tells her that is rude and that she is to call me Auntie. I am Miss Salter to everyone else. But to get on with the point—when Sheila says I look so pretty, or whatever compliment she might give, her mother will blush and say, "Isn't she naughty? I've been wanting to tell you that, but of course did not, and now she comes right out and says it." I shall have to ask her sometime whether it is considered rude to say a dress is pretty or a ring beautiful. I have been doing that whenever I felt the urge—which unfortunately is not very often in light of the clothes these English women wear. I do know that I cause quite a furor when I put my soft boiled egg in a cup and then add pepper, salt, and butter, and even a chunk of bread. They have never heard of eating an egg that way, much less seen it done in "polite society."

They tease me about my accent, but I think it is done in a friendly way, for they really fall over backwards not to offend. Mrs. O'Neil told me that I was the saving grace during the first teatime on board because I initiated conversation with them. I have to laugh at this, for I was using such restraint I was bursting. I wanted to introduce myself and tell them to call me Kate and rush around welcoming them to the *Mongolia*.

Sensing the English fear of intrusion, I just barely asked that the tea be passed—and they call this friendship! I seem to be the greatest tea drinker on board, which is a surprise to us all. I'm the only one who has it for breakfast.

The Captain—and I must get around to a description of him soon, for he is the Captain to end all captains—had a cocktail party on the King's birthday. Sadly enough I took to my bed immediately afterwards and missed a banquet which the King himself probably did not have. The stewards were so upset at my absence that they kept popping in to urge food on me. At the end of the dinner they came in a group with a huge platter of ice cream, a bottle of wine, and a table decoration which is the most beautiful I have ever seen. It is an ice swan about a foot high. It had a tiny light beneath it and was surrounded by flowers. You can't imagine how ethereal this looks in a dark room. I think that the Christmas festivities will be something unbelievable on this ship. Also, we are developing a very nice feeling of friendship which should be very homey by Christmas time.

Our real humor comes from Mr. Price. His tales of the concentration camp are curiously funny beyond belief. He is very much like the gay young blood (grown a little older) in the P. G. Wodehouse books. Some afternoon when we are sailing through the middle of the Indian Ocean and I haven't any vital news to write, I shall try to recount some of his stories of camp life.

Mrs. W. continues her incessant talking. I want you people to please write to me at once and tell me if I have this weakness. If I have, it is almost worse than B.O. and I must do something about it. She absolutely monopolizes every conversation. Since we are all so polite on board, there is no person with whom I can discuss this catastrophe and at least have the fun of knowing that I am not alone in my frantic boredom. I need all of my willpower not to put my ear to the wall when the Prices retire for the night (they are in the next room) and hear whether they let out a wild gasp of relief as they close their door behind them after one of her hour-long monologues in the drawing room.

Last night it was Peter's foot rot! (Apparently the English version of athlete's foot!) We've gone through bed linen, Peter's height, Peter's manliness, English rations, Peter's mustache, Peter's weight, Peter's helplessness, Peter's skill at engineering, Iraq-this, Iraq-that, and on and on until time at last runs out. It is doubly maddening since Mr. Price is just as anxious to talk as Mrs. Warren and his stories are so wonderfully funny that I feel robbed to have to miss a single one of them.

I have discovered one thing about the women on board. Each of us has a profession. Mrs. O'Neil was a nurse in the war. Mrs. Rackham was a supervisor of some chain department store. Mrs. Price was a music teacher, as well as a teacher of English and journalism in China, and Mrs. Warren was a bacteriologist who tested London's sour milk. (Can you imagine such a job!)

A new woman boarded the ship in Marseille. I think she may be the long awaited missionary. No one has told me this, but certainly a ship bound for the Orient must carry at least one reformer. She is the other "Miss" aboard and she is English, stocky, and has small features, frizzed short hair, a manly walk, tailored suits, and a comradely air about her.

Mrs. W. and I had a rather heated discussion on humor. She said she found the English sense of humor was so much more subtle than ours. "Nothing like *Punch*, don't you know?" she said. Fortunately, I have some *New Yorkers* with me, so they can win my case without any further comment from her.

I must have a quick nap before "tiffin" so I shall put these pages aside. I adore this journal idea, for it is like having a long cozy conversation with my favorite people and it is unique in that I can plan every subject we'll talk about and hear absolutely no argument to any of my ideas…not that I mind a good argument every now and then!

17 December 1949—At Port in Genoa

Today was a day of days! Rarely have I had such an utterly perfect day! It began before dawn when I heard the deep blast of our ship's horn announcing our arrival in Genoa. I struggled sleepily with myself as to whether it was more heavenly to sleep or to peer out my porthole and watch the city of Genoa as we approached it. Sleepy as I was, my sense of obligation made me stick my head out of the porthole, and there were the "hills of Genoa." Set in inky blackness with sparkling lights scattered all about, and the first glimmer of daylight was just barely touching the sky. It was pure magic, and I sank back into bed with a sigh of contentment. Not for long, however, for the sturdy Italian tugs hooted and shrilled and screamed at our ship, the harbor ships, and each other. In addition, the steward knocked loudly to tell me that the princess was about to be discharged with pomp. After ignoring these interruptions to the best of my ability, the steward came again with tea, and I was up for the day.

I went out into the early morning light and watched flowers and counts and royalty galore mingling with the curious stevedores. I watched our Captain barking orders to the sailors to make the lower deck fit for a preliminary funeral, and I watched a dapper Italian gentleman descend to the hold. More than that I could not stomach, so I went in for a hearty breakfast while the others ooh-ed and aah-ed at the crane and its solemn burden.

Gabriel O'Neil, "Gay," and I set out to see the sights of Genoa after breakfast, and everything about the day seemed right as we eyed the huge ships, rough looking stevedores, donkey-drawn cargo carts, and near-by hills with the city of Genoa scattered about on them.

After changing our money, we set out for the Via Luccoli which had been recommended to us as a tiny, atmospheric, old-city shopping street. It was marvelous to be back in Italy again, for that has always been a wonderful dream to me. Even my misery has been a romantic, happy kind of misery in Italy, and I associate an intense joy with this country. The smells were the smells I remembered and shop windows full of exquisite silver, leather, and silks. I only changed ten dollars, but I felt like a millionaire with my sixty thousand liras in my purse and only luxuries to spend them on.

Gay and I found such streets as I cannot believe even exist in the casbah. They were not more than a yard and half wide, cobble-stoned, and bordered by high, dark buildings. Every few feet would be an intersection even darker and narrower with tiny steps leading up into slums filthy beyond description. Wash hung from all levels suspended by ropes across the streets. Cows hung by their feet in open markets. White, slimy octopus slithered about shop windows; prawns, crabs, clams, and oysters were displayed, as well as cheese, sausages, coral, baskets, perfumes, sponges, pastries, chianti bottles in wicker baskets, cameos, hot chestnuts—everything—to the end of the world!

Sprinkled about this setting of cobblestones, dirty wash, and fish smells were people by the hundreds all looking like overdone characters on an MGM set. There were tarts, old bearded rabbis, beggars in black capes, young hoodlums who went wild with delight when I took their pictures, buxom housewives doing their marketing for the day, ogling little girls with heavy black pigtails, slimy unshorn loafers with a leer and foul language (in Italian, thank heavens!), bohemian students and young artists, chintzy shop girls, old crones huddled in black shawls, clinging young couples looking significantly at one another, and through all of this, Kate and Gay whisking along with utter amazement and delight. One English-speaking Italian man brushed up to us and said in an Oxford accent, "This is no place for two ladies such as you. You take the first street to the left and get out of here at once!" And with that he stood in attendance to see whether we followed his advice. We did not. It was far too exciting and anyway we felt that there was safety in numbers and never had I been in such crowds.

After looking and looking and never deciding what to buy, we suddenly came upon a jewel shop with jagged coral necklaces in the window. We dashed in and found just what we had been looking for. A most domineering old tyrant thrust them at us when suddenly I spied some Venetian necklaces. I have longed for one ever since Palmer came back from Venice with one of the most exquisite, pastel colored string of beads I have ever seen. The price was one tenth of what I thought it would be and I went absolutely wild. It was like being in Tiffany's with an unlimited charge account. I was dashing around this two-by-four shop from rack to rack pulling out gold, turquoise, pale pink, scarlet, and royal blue Venetian beads. Three times we left the store and had it locked behind us (Saturday noon) and three times we found another treasure in the window and knocked frantically for admission one more time. Finally, when we had only six hundred lira left between us, we departed.

We were famished by now, and we went in search of the real McCoy in Italian restaurants. We found a perfect little spot called Ristorante Toscana. For six hundred lira we had two steaming hot plates of spaghetti, a bottle of red wine, and rolls; I have rarely enjoyed a meal so much. We were radiant, we had walked for miles, we were starved, we were in love with everything we had bought (and of course unwrapped bundles exclaiming over each of them during lunch), and we were thoroughly enjoying each other's company. I am the first American Gay had ever known, and I always find this a delightful challenge. I am sure we will be fast friends by the end of the voyage, and she has repeatedly asked me to come to visit her in Singapore, which is not too fantastic a thing to happen at all.

Her husband, as I have mentioned before, has been hired by the Malay government to be in charge of the anti-bandit movement, and so it ought to be a most interesting experience.

Gay volunteered the information that she is delighted with my voice and thinks that I speak almost with an English accent.

I mention this only because I was beginning to fear opening my mouth lest my voice sound too terrible to my British shipmates. Often in stories they will imitate an American and I always cringe because it sounds so apt and so nasal.

Being utterly broke, we started walking back to the ship, which was miles away. It turned out that this walk cost us ten dollars because we passed a store with the most lushly beautiful angora sweater sets I have ever seen. I tried one on "just for the fun of it," and was talked into buying it by Gay. It has really been ages since I have just spent money on myself helter-skelter—aside from investments such as my Leica—so it was with a sense of delicious abandonment that I told the man to "wrap it up." I wore a string of pearls and a new sweater to dinner tonight and the English reserve at last broke down and there was wild exclaiming from everyone. Mr. Price was so frantic about it that he dashed to his wife's cabin and wanted to whisk her into town at once to buy her a set. He was willing to find the storekeeper's house and take him to his store in a taxi if need be to be sure that his darling little blonde wife would have a sweater set like mine.

We all had fun displaying our purchases of the day and gasping with delight at the mosaic work, cameos, silk scarves, and other treasures. I feel as though I have walked into a child's fairyland. I have spent a lot of money in the past three years, but never with such sheer gaiety and carefreeness as today. I have already bought a few presents which will be winging their way to each person reading these pages. The Prices have told me that Port Said is even more irresistible, so heaven help my purse there! Maybe you'll only have one present each, but that present will be a perfect one—no matter how small. I want it not only to be something lovely to have, but a constant reminder of the fact that dreams do come true.

The whole atmosphere of the ship has altered. It is a thousand times more jovial and comradely now. The Prices and I had a cocktail before dinner and a marvelous conversation. It is the first time we have had a talk alone and I really enjoyed it. We three are planning to do Bangkok together, as we will be the only ones left on board by then. We had great fun planning the exploration. The Captain has suggested that I wire ahead to the American Embassy and have them meet our launch and take us into Bangkok proper. I am going to try to work this out through the Singapore Embassy on the grounds of being a journalist.

The Prices have asked me to play golf with them in Singapore at "the lovely course there, by jove!" I laugh aloud to myself in my bunk just thinking of Kate on a golf course in Singapore with a rousing round on the links followed by a "You must have a Singapore Sling in the ripping club there!" What a fantastic dream I'm in the midst of!

After each little cluster went their way tonight, the Captain joined the Prices and me for conversation; he is one of the most unique people I have ever met in my life. I shall try to do justice to him by word and photograph, but I think that even a Shakespeare Wolf would fail (for the benefit of you laypeople, Wolf is the leading Leica man). I am, however, too tired to tackle this undertaking tonight. It is late, late, late, and I must go to bed…though not to sleep because I am too happy.

So far I've heard no Christmas carols at all. I just can't let Christmas come and go unnoticed, and so I sing carols softly to myself at night in my bed, hoping that the Prices don't hear me next door. Good night.

20 December 1949—On the blue, blue Mediterranean off the coast of Italy

We are sailing again! It is amazing how you grow used to the gentle vibrations of the ship's motor and the slight motion of the ship itself and how very much you miss this in port. Last night I really slept for the first time in three nights, just because of the comforting feeling of moving again.

Today is like a preview. I'm in my peasant shoes, no stockings, cotton skirt and cotton blouse. Mrs. Price is wearing white shoes, Mr. Price has an ascot tie and short-sleeved navy blue shirt with no jacket, and Mrs. Warren announced that she has removed her woolly vest (some ungodly kind of undergarment that the English wear). The sea is absolutely flat. Even the disturbance the ship causes as it pushes ahead barely ripples the surface. Italy and Sardinia lie close beside us and we are heading for the Straits of Messina (between the toe of the boot and Sicily). The sun is warm and golden and, although the air is briskly cool, in a few days it will just be luxurious warmth and brightness. Never have I felt so smug. I react to winter as though it were a personal enemy, and I feel that after twenty-seven years of submission, I have at last turned the tables on that freezing, hostile person and I am absolutely preening with delight.

Another feeling I have now is of the most delicious expectancy in the world. Up until now—Rotterdam, Antwerp, Marseille and Genoa—these places were places I was seeing for a second time. Now I am pushing into the great unknown and long-awaited Middle East and Far East. I have conflicting desires. One feeling is that of urgency. I want to see these places as soon as possible. The other feeling is that I want every minute to go slowly and be treasured and to have the trip take a lifetime. In every way this experience is a fulfillment of the most complete sort. It is really heaven on earth.

Our group has at last jelled. Although we are each very different people and only one or two of us might seek each other out on land, we are all fitting together beautifully at sea. Some of the people who have traveled a lot by ship (and this is Mr. Price's eighth voyage along this route) say this is the most congenial collection of passengers they have ever encountered. Mr. Price also said that this ship is the most comfortable and the most thoroughly enjoyable of any ship he has ever sailed on.

Even Mrs. Warren is calming down a bit. I think it is because, by silent agreement, we refuse to be bullied into listening to her monologues anymore. There is politeness, yes. But I notice that Mr. Price will ever so quietly interrupt her by starting a conversation with the person to his left, and Mrs. Price pretends that she doesn't hear her at all, and Mrs. Rackham takes advantage of Mrs. Warren's stopping to cough by moving right along with her own story. Now that each of us is feeling more relaxed and normal, we will not be silenced altogether, and this more even balance of conversation makes life happier and more interesting.

I have a messy little scrap of paper with various words jotted down at random which are supposed to get me off on a variety of subjects. I'll run through some of these topics in a helter-skelter manner. One thing which is utterly delightful is that in every port we are presented with roses and carnations and what have you with the compliments of The East Asiatic Shipping Company.

Our new passengers have come aboard. They will be excellent subjects for photographs. There is an elderly Chinese couple. The man, Mr. Li, an author of some repute, has been teaching geology at Oxford under an exchange professorship. He and his wife are exquisite, quiet bits of what the Orient is like at its best. Then there is a slight, young (twenty-six), beautiful German-Japanese girl with her two children. She has been living in Germany for the past thirteen years and is traveling with her children—ages four and five. She has apparently divorced her husband and is now going back to her family in Japan.

The most obnoxious of the passengers is a young, swarthy, bombastic Filipino who has just taken his Master's Degree at Michigan and now calls himself "Doctor." His is going back to lead a group in Public Health in Manila. He is the kind of man who stares at you significantly, which makes me livid with rage. I am polite, but ignore him as much as possible. He speaks very loudly with American affectations. He is obviously overjoyed that I am a single American girl bound for Manila, too, but he has definite disappointment in sight if he thinks that fact is going to affect his life in any way. He may prove nice eventually, but he has gotten off to quite a blatant start.

There is also a stocky English woman named Miss Deans, a government employee who has decided to travel. She has taken a civil service job as secretary to the governor of North

Borneo and is on her way to the East with a two-year contract. In a way, it is rather the same step I took when I first came to Germany. I admire her for doing it, but I am so grateful that, for the moment at least, that kind of experience is over for me and that I am going to join Dockie, my father, in Manila as a daughter and a loafer for a while. I'm not too keen on reaching into an unknown country for a job and taking whatever comes your way. I'd like to pick my own job, if and when I have to do this again.

What is most wonderful is the feeling of again being a human being. In Germany, every element seems to be working to convince you that you are a downtrodden, undesirable, untouchable human being. A typical example is that although people can be nice to you at Rhein-Main, they never think of carrying that courtesy to the point of inviting you to their home. The idea of asking you to come over to meet their family and have dinner in a home atmosphere, sitting around the living room for normal conversation, is unthinkable. After a while, you feel that such an act *is* unthinkable. You feel that there must be something wrong with you and that you are not fit to meet a wife or a mother or a sister or a child. It is quite terrible the way single girls in Germany are simply left to shift for themselves as best they can, and, with startlingly few exceptions, they are never invited to cross the boundary from working girl to "friend-in-the-home." I find that there is a deep, deep hurt in me because of this and it is a behavior I cannot forgive of the American people in the Occupation. No matter how dense the person, he must realize what it would mean to a girl who is thousands of miles away from her family and friends to be shown a kind of warmth which has nothing to do with the office. If I am ever in a position to share my home life with someone who does not have any, I am going to fall over backwards to do so. I think it is selfish and insensitive and cruel for those who have a family life to hoard it from those to whom an occasional glimpse of a home would mean so much.

This past year was very important to me both emotionally and financially. But never again am I going to put myself into such an alien society. Under the mantle of the generous acceptance and interest and friendliness of the passengers aboard the *Mongolia*, I am beginning to feel like Kate Salter again. It is too good a feeling to ever give up. I am, as it were, regaining my identity. I think that this is one reason I was so eager for mail in Germany, for with each letter from you, I felt like me, instead of that queer recluse I was forced to become in Rhein-Main. However—enough of all that. The point is that life is civilized and kind and outgoing now, and it is an atmosphere which permeates one's being and lifts away the worries and cares and grief which one may have. Right now, I can't imagine anyone more carefree and optimistic or radiant than I am!

As we begin to know each other on the *Mongolia*, there is more give and take, and easy exchange of ideas and such. One of the most tempting things which is happening is that Mrs. Price (who has been in the Orient for the last ten years) is beginning to shyly bring from her cabin things that she has bought there. This is like something out of the Arabian nights. There are black pearl earrings, jade necklaces and earrings, rough pearls set in dainty nests of gold, frothy feminine lingerie, richly brocaded evening jackets lined with the exquisitely soft wool of new-born lambs, and gold and silver-threaded satins and taffetas that you cannot believe are real. Best of all, there is the fact that the prices seem unbelievably low. The Orient must be a magic never-never land. Not only are there tangible things like opium dreams of the most ethereal world, but the description of the people, the country, the way of life, the pace of life, all sounds like perfect happiness. My reaction now is that I shall never leave the Far East. And the nice part is, if I feel that way after I arrive there, and wish it strongly enough, I never have to leave.

That is one of the magic charms of this adventure. Not only am I having the glorious experience of the ship, the ports, the fresh sea air, the food (and I have gained at least five pounds), *but* I have the mysterious unknown of what life will be like after I finally arrive. Gay O'Neil is fascinated with my lot (she knows nothing about me—my past, or my present, or my hopes for the future). She never tires of describing the absolute rarity of a single white girl. She describes such an aura of worship and attention and parties and dancing and golf and swimming and driving, that I just cannot believe she means that I am the person who will be in the center of all of this. Not only does she describe it, but she is planning which dashing young bachelors she will have waiting for me at the dock in Singapore when I arrive for a visit to her home. You know that I don't really care so much about this, but you can still imagine what fun it is to hear someone eagerly think and talk about such things for you.

I have now bought several presents for you. I was so pleased with my shopping on Saturday that when Monday came around I shot back into town before the ship left and bought some more lovelies. Something absolutely shouted Betsy to me, so that will go to Santa Fe as soon as possible. I found a little delectable which will be perfect for Hannah and am only sorry I shan't be able to see it on her. Also, I found several other treasures which seem to be arguing back and forth about whom they should go to. I'll figure it all out by the time I get to Manila and mail the bundles via the Navy so I know you will receive them duty-free.

If any of you are longing for something special from this part of the world, now is the time to voice your request. Otherwise you shall have to put your trust in the art of the Middle and Far East, the taste of KSS, and the Salter budget. I have allotted a certain amount of dollars just for happy spending and while I am within that limit I am going to pretend I am a millionaire with no thought of being broke. When I reach the end, I shall decide what the next step will be—but not until then. Enough about money...

I don't mind saying that I am expecting quite a bit of mail in Port Said. I have put myself in your shoes and decided that, were I you, that is the place I would send the first letter (notice that I said "first"). It is now Tuesday and we arrive there on Friday. Apparently we will be in the Suez Canal for Christmas.

East Asiatic Company Brochure

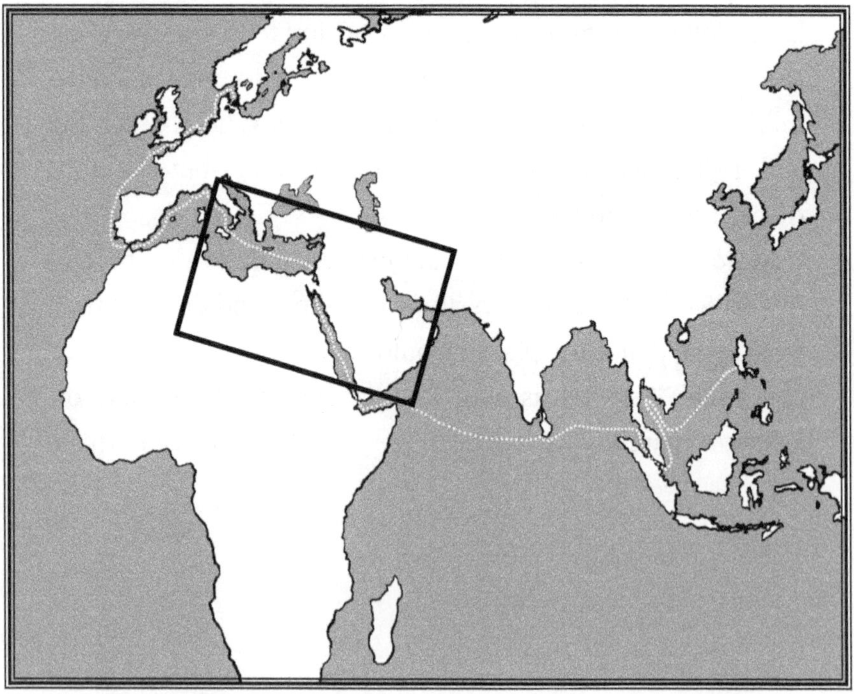

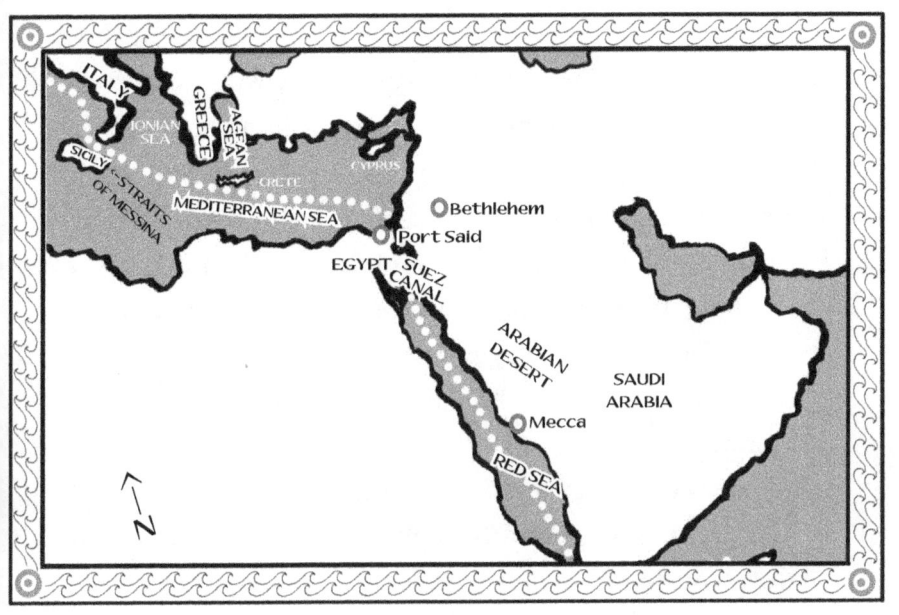

Watching Stars Come out of the Dark Blue Sea

21 December 1949 (first day of Winter)
South of the Island of Crete in the Mediterranean

I've just come from a bath of hot salty water. As I splashed about in the luxurious warmth, I rapturously admired bronzed arms (mine)! I thought, "At long last! The first day of winter and Kate has the beginning of a glorious tan!" I get tremendous enjoyment from the idea that all of this golden sun is stolen, and that really I should be sniffling and wheezing through winter slush under frozen skies. Now I bask in delight every second on this voyage.

Yesterday, as we headed south along the coast of Italy, we steadily felt the change in temperature. I was able to don a cotton skirt and strapless top and I spent the day on a deck chair really purring in the sun. Today was even better and from nine until about three-thirty I didn't budge from a salty corner of the deck which combined spray, sun, open railing, and the vista of miles and miles of blue sea. The Mediterranean is living up to its international reputation of "blue, blue, blue," and added to this is a surface as calm as a mill pond. It is a luxury cruise at this point, and waiters bring us lemonade and cold beer as we bask beneath the long awaited sun.

Yesterday was wonderful not only because of the sun. In the evening we passed Stromboli. That is a small island with a constantly erupting volcano. It was velvet black against the softer black horizon, and from the top of this jagged mountain of an island sprayed rose-gold lava which illuminated all the space around it. At times the volcano looked like a huge bonfire, but when it erupted it was similar to a super-colossal show of fireworks.

A few hours after we left Stromboli behind, we came to the Straits of Messina. We saw the lights of Italy and the lights of Sicily and they looked as though they were joined, they were so close together. Somehow the ship was guided deftly through and suddenly the lights were on either side of us and we had found the Straits.

By then it was midnight and I sleepily went back to bed and thought, "Now we are just coming into the Ionian Sea and the Aegean Sea is not far away, and it is the first day of winter and yet it is only a cool, friendly night—not cold and hideous." The evening star last night came out with the brilliance of a wonderful diamond when the sky was still a light blue with a rosy pink horizon below. It looked the way the star of Bethlehem looks in Christmas cards. When I looked at my map, I saw that we are very close to Bethlehem and it might well have been the Star of Bethlehem. Later, as the sky grew darker, I saw more stars than I have ever seen in my life. There were wide belts of milky way, planets, stars, and stardust. Several of the stars had wide paths of silver reflecting on the sea below they were so bright. The Chief Mate came up to me after dinner as I was looking at all of this out on the deck and said it was the most amazing clearness he has seen on this sea in years and years.

    I wore my new exquisitely soft, fluffy angora sweater last night. It was the feeling of walking into an unbelievable storybook to stand at the deck railing in this feminine, expensive, beautiful sweater and smell my wonderful perfume, hold a lacy handkerchief, and feel the cool wind blowing back my hair from my sunburned face, watch the stars come out of the dark blue sea, and know that it was Kate doing this, and she is heading into an unknown future in the Orient which hopefully will be wonderful. (This sentence is badly strung together, but I've included the ingredients which show what a dream world I'm living in now. Both my brain and my fingers are a little sunburned, and this writing doesn't go so well in the tropical setting.) It is just that everything is as it should be. I can't believe there ever was a war, that I lost the love of my life, that I ever was broke, or even unhappy. For the moment, life is just sea and wind and sun with hors d'oeuvres, tea, clean sheets, dressing for dinner, and friendly people. By the time I reach Manila, I suppose I won't mind leaving it all behind, but at the moment I find that I just want time to stand still.

24 December 1949—Noon—Suez Canal

Tomorrow is Christmas Day and I think it will be one of the happiest I have ever had. Our group is warm and friendly, and real affection has developed amongst us, so that each person will be going out of his way to see that the others have a marvelous Christmas.

Last night we arrived at Port Said, Egypt. We anchored in the harbor and small motor launches darted about us with pompous, dirty Arab officials complete with red fezzes and white gloves. I took a picture of one particularly languid looking young man who was motoring past us. He pulled his boat up to ours, came aboard and sought me out, and told me it was forbidden to take pictures in the harbor. BUT since I had taken his picture, here was his address, and would I please mail him a copy. In return he promised to mail me some pictures of Egyptian mosques.

After the rigamarole of officials looking at our passports and men coming aboard to change our money, we finally all boarded a small row boat named "Moses" and Moses himself rowed us ashore!

We headed for Simon Artaz, a waterfront store which is very plush and touristy. In a twinkling of an eye it was time to get back on board for dinner and everyone prepared to rush back to Moses. I just couldn't. I had seen no more of Egypt than one store, and we had until ten at night before we sailed. Fortunately, Peggy Deans, the other "Miss" on board, wanted to see Port Said, too, so amidst the pleadings of the others to "be careful" we stayed. I had a few misgivings because, on the whole, I would say Egyptians are the most cutthroat people in the world. But, on the other hand, how many times does one get to Egypt in a lifetime?

So Peggy and I had three hours of roaming around Port Said. It was night and everything had a special aura of excitement, sparkle, color, and atmosphere about it. We ambled up and down the main street past the dirtiest, smelliest, most picturesque people I have ever seen. An election was going on and a politician arrived in a sleek American car. He was whisked out onto the shoulders of the mob and then into a gaudily decorated pavilion. Loud speakers were connected to the street and Arab wailing and chanting filled the air. Everywhere there were rags, turbans, trailing robes, olive faces, evil eyes, smells, pushy merchants accosting you with silver, jade, ivory, and accents of untold description and kinds.

I bought three lace handkerchiefs (which I have learned don't keep their shape when they are ironed), one perfume flacon that leaks, two used Indian blouses that smell, and a "pure silver" bracelet which is tin, plus some Yardley's, which is always good. I tried the blouses on when I got back on board and imagined I had scabies all night long. However, once fumigated and mended, these blouses will be the dream of any artist. They are covered with tiny mirrors and embroidered in plums, fuschias, purples, and deep reds. All in all, I suppose I was taken for a prize fool by the Egyptian merchants, but this is the land where the inevitable happens, and one is not a real traveler until it has happened to her thoroughly at least once.

The only really disturbing part of all this is that my cabin smells today, and I have a sneaking suspicion it is the blouses. Too bad. I thought they were such dreams when I saw them in the dark of the store.

When we finally returned to the waterfront, Moses was waiting for us, and how relieved I was to see him, for I didn't want to trust us to some unknown Arab who might row us off to a red light district and keep us there forever. There was an Italian luxury liner which had just pulled into the dock and it was big and shining and full of people and music and all the sound effects and travelogue folders enticing readers to see the world. I adored seeing it, but I felt that our beautiful ship out in the harbor was the real queen of ships, and I wouldn't trade places with any passenger on a luxury liner. It was a beautiful sight to be rowed at night past the many ships which were moored about.

As we finally pulled up to the gangway of the *Mongolia*, every single passenger was hanging over the railing, hailing us with delight. They had really been very worried, and never have I had such a homecoming. The stewards even had a meal waiting for us!

25 December 1949—
Red Sea—with the Arabian Desert on our starboard side and the city of Mecca approaching on the port side.

Merry Christmas! This is the first Christmas in years which has been a "merry" one for me, and though it is hot and I've heard almost no Christmas music this year, I really have the Christmas spirit.

Last night the East Asiatic Shipping Company gave us a Christmas Eve party we will not forget for years. There were cocktails at half past six and we all arrived in evening dress. Everyone looked lovely and extra special, and there was much exclaiming over our gowns. We all like each other to the point now where we appreciate the effort made to look pretty, even if the results aren't too glamorous. I wore a long black skirt and embroidered sequin shoes with my sequin sweater from Vienna. It was a striking ensemble.

After cocktails—with much toasting—we went in for a goose dinner. We had sparkling Burgundy and Madeira wine, a sweet rice dish which is always part of the Danish Christmas, potatoes, gravy, and rolls. We had a sweet Danish beer and finally a gorgeous layer cake. After dinner, we returned to the lounge and there was a small Christmas tree with candles, Danish flags, and tinsel. On the Victrola, marvelous Christmas hymns were playing. We had coffee, small cakes, and brandy. For several hours we sat around singing Christmas songs, and welcoming Santa Claus (the Chief Steward in quite an outlandish get-up), and looking at our presents. We had drawn names and each person had a small, beautiful thing from Genoa. My present is an exquisite, tiny jade vase. As the evening went on, we had scotch and soda and finally rum punch before we went to bed.

In the very early part of the evening, before cocktails, I had gone out to look at the evening star and to make a special wish upon it. There was a tiny slice of moon, the great shining evening star, and a pin point diamond of a star just below the evening star which made me realize how small all other stars are. It was a quiet and magical moment just realizing how near the Holy Land I was and seeing such a star shining in all its glory on Christmas Eve. The air was cool and fresh and the ship as steady as the most squeamish person could desire. I loved the feeling of leaning against the railing and realizing that I was entering the Red Sea and it was Christmas Eve and that life was so full and rewarding.

As soon as I had dressed for the evening I got out my tiny picture album which I carry in my purse and looked at each person's picture. Then, concentrating very hard on all of you, I toasted each of you, one by one, and downed a quick slug of cognac from my flask. By now it was night, and once again I went on deck to watch the stars and to think of each of you and of your lives.

After we had received our presents, I slipped away from the group to go back on deck, and saw one or two young sailors out there. Nearly all of the ship's crew are forbidden on our deck, but there is one cabin boy who looks very like brother Joel and who is at sea for the first time. He is often about. I've taken several pictures of him, and we have a budding friendship. He was looking rather wistful and was definitely happy to see me, so we had a Christmas talk. Several other young boys came up then, and it was great fun. They obviously find me quite exciting because I am an American girl and I am traveling alone. They always look at me most appreciatively in my various gay sunsuits and skirts, and I think they were quite entranced with my sparkling sequins and billlowing silk skirt. It was fun to feel that I was adding a bit to their Christmas. I know they added to mine.

Much later in the evening, after I had said goodnight to the party and started for my cabin, I decided to go on deck for just one more glimpse of the magic night. There was the young sailor and he looked absolutely thrilled to see me. I think he had been standing vigil for just this moment. He came up to me and said, "Miss, please don't go away. I want to give you a present." He dashed below and soon was back with a handkerchief wrapped around a rather bulky bundle. He unwrapped it, and there was a paperweight from Genoa. It was one of those lovely glass balls with a snowstorm inside. The object was a ship with a sea-blue atmosphere about it. The ship is that of Columbus, for Genoa was his home. I adore this present because it is all tied in with America, sailing, the young sailor, my great adventure, and this perfect Christmas. The boy was so happy to give it to me and I was really speechless with surprise.

I had one other present. Hannah gave me a box with instructions that it was not to be opened until Christmas Eve. Finally, on Christmas Eve afternoon, I couldn't wait another second. In it were some wonderful German cologne, a Christmas candle, and sprig of fir. Also, a most darling Christmas letter, telling me that if there wasn't a tree on board, then this fir could provide a tiny bit of Christmas atmosphere for me in my stateroom. It was a thoughtful, sensitive, touching present and I can't say how much I adored it. When I finally went to sleep last night, I was a happy, happy girl.

I won't elaborate on past Christmases, but I will say that last year I was alone in my room in Germany with a most ominous sense of worry about what the year would bring. The year before, I was stranded in that ghastly hotel in southern France waiting for Ivan and Babs to come and get me, which they didn't do until the following Christmas afternoon. And the year before that I was in Milan, alone, desperately miserable and with a drunken ensign. All in all, it has not been a happy time of year for me, but this year "all is right with the world!"

All day yesterday we traveled through the Suez Canal. It is a fascinating spot, for it is so narrow. There is definitely only room for one-way traffic, which I had never realized before. The coloring was truly Egyptian. The sand stretched for miles of pink-gold flatness. The sky was brilliantly blue with massive silver-white cold formations which hung low over the land. Camels dozed by the stone embankment of the canal. Arabs shuffled along in heavy white robes. Women passing by stared at us even though they had jugs balanced on their heads. There were a scattering of tents, swimming beaches, and occasional plush clubs or hotels. Several ancient rafts with oddly shaped sails went by in a slow procession. Ahead of us and behind us were other huge ships in our convoy. Halfway, we had to pull out of the canal into the Bitter Lakes to let traffic go by in the other direction. Off our starboard side, I recognized the *Tuscana*, which was the huge luxury liner I had seen in Port Said the night before. All through the day, as I saw these sights and as I joined the Prices in a friendly beer or talked to Peggy Deans (with whom I am striking up a really warm friendship), I kept trying to make myself realize the full impact of what I was doing. I was sailing through the Suez Canal! I just can't believe this trip is real. Each morning when the steward comes in with my morning tea, I pop up to look out the porthole. Always there are rosy clouds, delicious seas, and wonderful names to say, such as "Good morning, Red Sea"…or, "Hello, Ionian Sea," and soon the Arabian Sea and the Indian Ocean and the Isthmus of Kra. I think this trip has convinced me of magic, of a dream world, of wishes coming true, or young dreams materializing. It is one of the great, great experiences of my life, and I shall always bear the stamp of it.

This is a wonderful taste of getting along with people and getting to know other people. I adore being the only American, and I sense that, to nearly all of these people, Americans are thought to be queer beings. They expect us to be rude, to be loud, to be greedy. They also expect us to be dashing and unusual and overwhelming. They aren't too sure they'll like us. They think we will be rich and lordly. It is really fun to feel that I am winning over the passengers and the officers and the crew. In spite of my cameras—which make me look contemptuously rich—I think they have all decided they are very glad to know me. And I think in future discussions about Americans, many of these people will say, "Well, I met an American girl once who wasn't like that…." I adore being an ambassador for my country, and the more I see of the world, the prouder I am to belong to that country.

Peggy Deans may eventually be a very fast friend of mine. She is the sad sort of person who is deeply feminine on the inside but looks bulky and solid on the outside. I find her wistfully staring at the exquisite Japanese girl and struggling with envy. She is absolutely taking the bull by the horns in taking this two-year job as secretary to the governor of Borneo, and I admire her courage tremendously. I was grateful for that courage too, when she said she would stay with me in Port Said, for we had a marvelous time seeing that town together. She has never traveled at all, and it is amusing and darling to see her eagerness and her shyness and her talkativeness all mixed together when we do business with shopkeepers or bargain with wandering street merchants. She considers me the experienced and knowing traveler and although I know how wrong she is, it is flattering and fun to have her look to me for the final word and action in so much of what we do. Since Borneo is so close to Manila, I wouldn't be at all surprised if I went to visit her. I know I shall visit the Prices in Japan, for they are a most charming and humorous couple, and more and more we have private conversations together as we are planning our days in Singapore and Bangkok.

Mr. Price is absolutely overwhelmed by my Egyptian blouses. He thinks them daring and full of history. He is sure that dancing girls owned them previously. And he can't imagine that I'll ever wear them in public. Gay O'Neil, on the other hand, thinks them terribly unsanitary, but divinely beautiful and thinks they are real treasures. There is no doubt that they stink! I have doused them in mothballs, covered them in newspaper, and put them in the farthest corner of a suitcase I could find. On the whole, I am glad I got them. I examined my purse flacon carefully. There was tiny writing on it and I dreaded reading it, for I feared it would say USA. Fortunately it was Czechoslovakian.

27 December 1949—The Red Sea

It is with a cozy sense of homecoming that I sit down to the forty-fourth page of this journal. Never have I had such real joy from writing as on this trip. I don't know why I didn't start a journal years ago, for it makes the ideal living companion since I can't be with any one of you on this expedition. For the rest of the trip I am going to try to concentrate more on the actual phrasing of sentences and choice of words. Up until now I have always had too many ideas racing through my head in bold color to paint the picture I have in mind. The one thing I am afraid of when you long-suffering people read this is that I will tell you more about freighters than you care to know! However...

At the moment there are so many things to say I don't quite know which tangent to select. I think I'd better begin with Mrs. Warren and the Captain. By the way, Mr. Price has tabbed Mrs. Warren so perfectly that I lay awake at night laughing at his description. According to him, "that young lady has been injected with a gramophone needle."

The Captain of this ship just about defies description. He is Prussian to the nth degree. He is tall, broad, fair, fifty-ish, roaring, dogmatic, tyrannical, amusing, pig-headed, interesting, domineering, very religious, and highly entertaining. He brooks no argument whatsoever, and if you try to respond to his comments, he will say slowly and deafeningly, "I beg your pardon, Madame." With that comment he will draw himself up in his chair and scowl so fiercely in your direction that you tremblingly sink down into your chair. If you had to live with this man or work with him it would be insufferable. But for a nearly seven-week pleasure cruise he is marvelous. We all delight in his fantastic stories of other trips and other passengers and allow ourselves to be pretty thoroughly bossed around by him.

All of us, that is, except Mrs. Warren. She reminds me of several years ago, when I believed that you must always declare your every intention and belief immediately and loudly and then prepare to defy all opposition. Now I understand the value of timing and of slowly building up your ideas, convincing your opponent bit by bit. Mrs. Warren seems to feel a personal antagonism to the bossy ways of the Captain, and is determined to show him, to show herself and to show all of us that she is not one to be put down easily. The result is that she is disgracing herself, infuriating the Captain, and making it extremely uncomfortable, though interesting, for all the passengers.

Because she considers him not a gentleman, she is becoming "not a lady" in order to prove her point. It halfway looks as though she is trying to tempt him into doing physical violence to her so that she can relish the conflict and then report it later to the company, thereby ruining the Captain's career. The frigid disgust of the other passengers as this drama unravels is something to behold. There is no one like an Englishman to quietly and effectively "give you the ice."

Unfortunately, Mrs. Warren picked Christmas Day to bring matters to a head. After lunch on that day, she and the Captain stayed in the dining room drinking until nearly four o'clock. The result is that they both got drunk, quarrelsome, and a bit maudlin. The Captain wrenched her neck a little, according to Peggy, who saw the episode, and who observed that Mrs.W. more than asked for it, and she in turn tweaked his nose, which created a scarlet gash on it, still evident to all of us. (What the crew must think, I do not know. He is such an unapproachable and terrifying man that for them to know that he has had his nose scratched by a lady passenger must make them roar with delight.)

For the rest of the afternoon, Mrs. Warren wandered around the hallways mumbling about drinking the Captain under the table—which she indeed did, to the horror and amazement of us all—and that he couldn't rule her, and that she was a lady, and so forth. The others absolutely shriveled up with disgust and we all felt a bit nervous as we arrived for the Christmas cocktail party at six-thirty. The Captain was most conspicuous by his absence. I heard the Chief Engineer trying to cajole Mrs. W. into taking it a little easy with the Captain. As I watched this conversation, I thought I'd give my right eye to hear the Chief Officer and the Chief Engineer discussing all of us. They probably have determined to treat her with gloves of the softest kid, for she could really ruin them at the rate she is going. After an unusually long cocktail hour, we went into dinner—still no Captain—and nearly jumped out of our shoes to see him sitting there at the head of the table. The vivid red of his nose was embarrassing to look at. Since I sit on his right, I had quite a burden of conversation and of attempting to act as though everything was just as it should be.

Our Christmas dinner was perfection, with red wine and Madeira wine and cordials in the lounge afterwards. Mrs. W. threw in a few incendiary remarks which the Chief Engineer, who sits at the foot of the table next to Mrs. W., did his best to drown out from his end, and which I did my best to bridge at my end. The expression of Mr. Price, who sits across the table from me, was worth a million dollars. He obviously has decided to enjoy this whole thing for what it is worth, and the sparkle in his eyes is wonderful to see.

I had a faint picture of the one-sidedness of the life of a passenger on this ship when the Captain told me that at that moment there was a crew member dying on board, and that just before dinner a sailor had come to him on the brink of suicide. This is a separate little world we are in, and it seems to have the same range of elements that the world on shore holds.

Unfortunately, the first dance the Captain had with Gay O'Neil, he fell under the Christmas tree. Much later, three of the women—led by Mrs. W.—tried to cut a button off of the Chief Officer's uniform, and the result is that they all fell in a heap in the cabinway. The steward commented to one passenger that, in his seventeen years at sea, never had he such a ghastly Christmas. I must confess that I took the maudlin with a grain of salt and I left the party early, so that all in all my memories are only beautiful. I went up to the top deck and stood for half an hour in an open little corner of the deck, looking at the moon and the Christmas star. I can think of no more heavenly place for thought than in the midst of a quiet sea on a moonlit night. It is the perfect place to sort out your thoughts and your hopes. Even if it becomes tearful, it has a magic charm to it which takes away the hurt.

Suddenly, I was aware that a young boy was beside me. I have mentioned two young sailors who are my favorites. They both remind me of brother Joel in spirit. One is the boy of Christmas Eve night who gave me the present and the other is the boy who met me the night I came on board. It was this latter boy who stood beside me. His pretext for conversation was to ask me how big Flushing, New York is, because he has a cousin living there. I don't think he ever listened for an answer, for we started off on a long and most interesting conversation which had nothing to do with Flushing. He really looked most adorable with his blond curly hair blowing in the wind and his hands thrust in his jacket pocket. Several of his friends went by once or twice in the night, and I know they are very jealous of whomever is talking to the American girl. I saw Johnnie, the boy who gave me the present, on the outskirts of the deck, and he looked most unhappy at this turn of events.

This young boy asked me to come up on the bridge, which is definitely forbidden. Since I knew the Captain was most securely anchored in the lounge below, I thought it the perfect time. He went up to ask the Third Officer who was standing watch. This Third Officer is the perfect picture of a young intelligent boy who has the secret goal of becoming a captain someday, and who is willing to do anything to achieve this. He is tall, slim, handsome, and looks a bit like Lawrence Olivier. He sent an invitation down at once, and so my young sailor glided ahead of me in the dark night saying "Follow me, Miss Salter." He vanished into the night.

I followed him up a narrow ladder and finally reached the famous bridge. It was something unbelievable. From this high and special place you can see for miles around. You feel almost up amidst the masts. The trembling lights from the bow and stern mast look very mysterious and beautiful as they make their way across the sea. The moon was a beautiful quarter-slice, and there were millions of tiny stars slightly separate from the big Christmas star. The young sailor vanished as soon as he had introduced me to the Third Officer and every now and then he would slip up to us to report that all was well and I need not fear being caught. I stayed there for half an hour talking about the sea and the life of a sailor and just looking. You can imagine how you would feel to be high above a moonlit sea (the Red Sea at that!), on Christmas night, standing on the bridge of a Danish cargo vessel and looking down upon masts and gantries and bow, feeling a gentle, salty wind about your hair and your face, and talking to a young, earnest Danish officer at your side.

It was a moment so full with happiness that I was almost unable to endure it. And part of me was looking at the picture of me, too. I had on my white silk off-the-shoulder blouse, a black silk skirt, and embroidered sequin slippers and an embroidered sequin belt. The light from the moon caught the sequins and made them sparkle like diamonds. I had a misty chiffon scarf from Italy, and it felt divinely glamorous as it blew about my throat. I seem to be going a bit overboard here, but I am trying to convey the picture of how fantastic it all seemed to me to feel young and attractive and expectant and happy after most of the feelings I have had in the past three years. It was like coming out of a hideous nightmare of dark and sordid things into a world that is too ethereal to be real at all. If my life ends this year, I'll feel as though it is no great loss, for so many wonderful things have happened to me that I can only rejoice at having been so lucky.

Just a moment ago, the Captain popped into my cabin wearing white shorts, white shirt, and a white tropical sun hat. He wanted to see how things were going with me, and I quailed indeed, for if he should pick up these pages and start reading, I'd have no way of preventing it. If he told us all to jump overboard, I think none of us would question such a command—except, of course, Mrs. W., and that would be the one time she was right! I've run out of paper now, and I pray to be able to buy some in Aden. We arrive there tomorrow.

The Flag of Denmark
flown Christmas Day on the MS *Mongolia*

East Asiatic Company Brochure

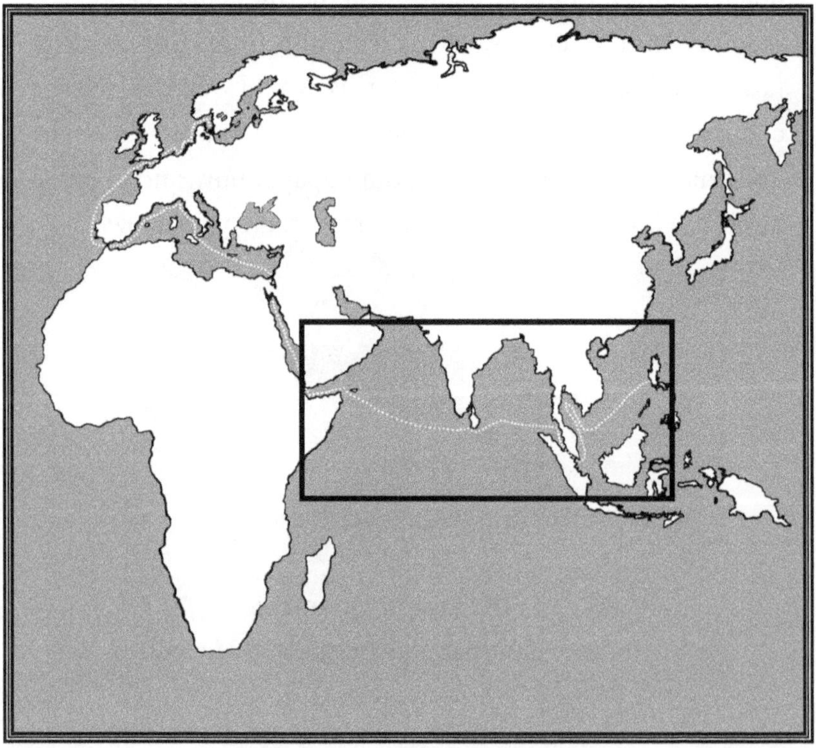

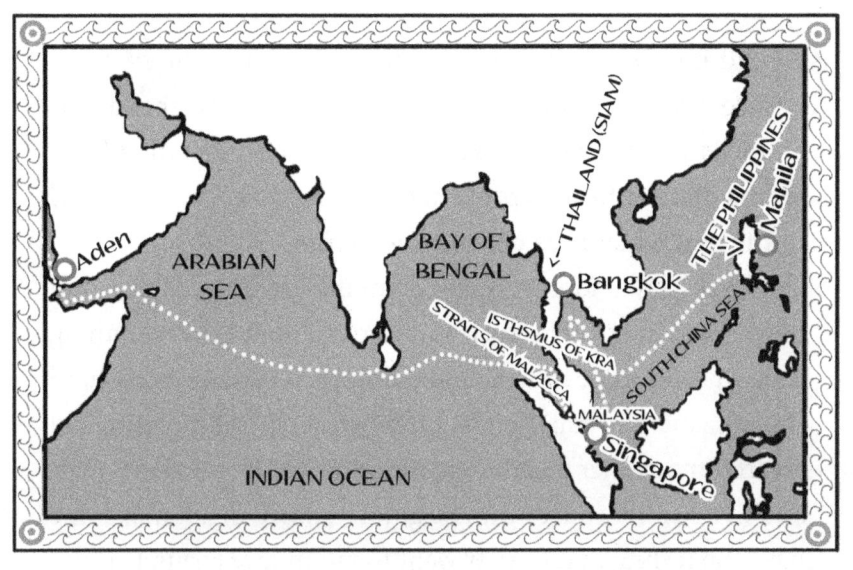

My Last Few Days as Rare Treasures

January 1950—Skirting the borders of the Arabian Sea and Indian Ocean near the Island of Ceylon.

In Aden the governor came aboard to speak to Gay. He brought the incredible, ghastly news that her husband was killed in an accident on Christmas Eve. These past days have been something unbelievable. It is one of the cruelest things in human nature that such grief cannot be shared by several, but has to be supported completely alone. I have learned something in courage in watching how she has taken this news. They were desperately in love, have absolutely no money, and had only been married for six years. Gay doesn't even have enough money to get back to England. She is going on to Singapore and may get a job as a nurse. Her whole future has suddenly been stripped of all happiness and turned upside down. Yet, in spite of this, after the first day or two, she has come to meals, she plays cards, she laughs and tells stories, and above all she protects her daughter from seeing that her heart is broken. I feel ashamed of my behavior in the past when I see her sheer guts now.

Since Gay and I were good friends before this dreadful news, I am the person she leans on most now, I do everything in my power to be of help and comfort. It is desperately hard though, and all I can do is to listen when she talks of him and try to convince her that the agonizing hurt will be less someday, and that life may once again be good in the living. It makes me have the feeling that I never want to fall in love again, because the penalty for losing that person is too great.

One of the things that will always stand us (the Salter kids) in such good stead is that our childhood was so radiantly happy. That is a bulwark against anything which may happen in the future. For Gay, her childhood was a nightmare, and now to be plunged into a future which holds only loneliness and absolutely no security is almost more than she can bear. I feel so sorry for her that I ache all over. Fortunately, I am so tired when I go to bed that I sleep, for otherwise the thoughts would be too unbearable. Whenever she feels like breaking down and telling me how she really feels, we go out on the deck and talk. I hope it is a relief to her, and it is something wonderful for me. I am just beginning to realize the debt I owe to Gil and the others around me in the years of 1946 and 1947. Though I can never repay them, I feel that I can square the debt a little by helping Gay. If any of you are taking your happiness for granted at the moment, think again.

Peggy Deans and I spend our mornings lying on top of the life boats in the open air. The spray, the sea, and the sun are something fantastically lovely. We talk and talk and talk. There are times when you meet a person and it does not seem as though you are American or English or what-have-you, but as though the two of you are a special breed apart. That is the way it is with Peggy and me. I think we shall be friends for life and I am thrilled about it. There are a million differences between the English and the American, and we talk about them with delight each day. We talk about our families, our spinsterhood, love, ship gossip, how we will bring up our children, what this next year may hold for us. This part of the trip couldn't be more fun.

On New Year's Eve I spent a lot of time by myself out on the top of the life boat. It is quite a thing to sit high on a ship and watch a full moon, a sky full of stars, and a calm Arabian Sea on the eve of 1950. The air was delectable and I am so golden brown and healthy now that I felt almost as though that evening were the very peak of my being. Much later, the crew invited Peggy and me down to their mess and the boy who plays the accordion came and we sang until four in the morning It was a wonderful, wonderful New Year's Eve in spite of the sorrow of Gay and the horror of Mrs. W.

Mrs. Warren and I had a final explosion on New Year's Eve. All evening Gay felt insecure and did not want to dampen the festivities. She took me aside to ask me if she was behaving alright. The strain was fantastic, since New Year's Eve is not a happy time at best, and for a woman whose husband has been killed less than a week earlier, it is a living hell. Gay was behaving marvelously and I told her so. For some reason this meant a great deal to her. I think the idea of hiding your feelings is so deeply ingrained in the British that they even find comfort in this, as well as great pride.

A few minutes before nine, Gay joined us in the lounge. Mrs. W. was sitting next to me and she whispered, "Kate, can you get Mrs. O'Neil out of here for a few minutes? At nine it will be midnight in Sumatra, and Mrs. Rackham and I want to toast our husbands."

I told her, "I don't see how I can get Gay out in any polite manner. Why don't you and Jo just look at each other at nine, and have a silent toast?"

Mrs. W. said this wouldn't do at all, since she wanted to have the three officers toast with her. Again, she asked that I get Gay out. I remembered how Gay had worried all night about her behavior and I knew if I suddenly said let's take a walk on deck, she would feel she was putting a damper on all of the rest of us. I told this to Mrs. W. So this boor of a woman said, "In that case, tell her the next five minutes will be very unpleasant for her and ask her to leave."

My blood was racing through my body so fast by now that I felt almost hysterical, and I shot Mrs. W. such a look as she will never forget. And then I heard the cruelest remark I have ever heard in my life. In an indignant and utterly spoiled voice Mrs. W. said, "Well, *my* husband is still alive, and I want to toast him." I left the room and we have not spoken since. I can't even look her in the eyes I hate her so. When you find someone that is so insensitive, then you begin to understand how concentration camps are possible. If she ever tries to broach this matter with me, I shall tell her this. But enough of that.

In Aden, after Gay heard the news, and then after a few hours, she asked me to go ashore with her. We hired a cab and drove through the filthiest, narrowest street I ever hope to see. Goats, cows, mongrel dogs, and pigs wander in and out of the three-sided houses where dozens of people live in one small room. The women wore long flowing gowns and many of them were heavily veiled so that their faces were invisible. There is terrific anti-Semitism; the Jews live on one side of the street and the Arabs on the other. We had done quite a bit of haggling about the price of our cab and finally had set it with a driver and a guide. This guide kept pointing to the Jews (who looked so much cleaner, more intelligent, and more civilized than the Arabs that there was just no comparison) and acting as though they were real untouchables Then, rather proudly, he pointed to a pile of filth saying that was the Arab section.

At the end of our journey, as we were approaching the docks, he told me not to try going into a Jewish store alone because it would be a dreadful experience. I asked him what would mark it off so and he said, "Because, Miss, they bargain and bargain and try and charge you much more than it is worth. You always have to argue with them."

"Oh," said I, "you mean the way we had to haggle with you over the fare of this cab." And he blushed. You cannot imagine how impossible it is to make an Arab blush. He looked both embarrassed and furious. I paid the driver and when this guide asked for a tip, I finally told him no.

We saw a very exciting thing on this trip. We went to Cleopatra's well and her reservoir. I must confess that it may not be hers, or it may have belonged to the Queen of Sheba, but whatever it was, it was absolutely brimming with antiquity and ghosts of the past. Aden is one of the hottest places in the world, and this well and reservoir were set in a perfect biblical backdrop. We stood at the bottom of sheer white cliffs which rose on three sides of us. The sky was brilliantly blue. The reservoirs hold twenty million gallons of water and are gouged out of the white cliffs in basins which finally reach the top. All around the tiny spot where we stood were flowers and small trees which formed next to the only oasis in Aden. Passing us from time to time were impish boys chattering like mad for tips, shy little girls, women heavily shawled and veiled, and turbaned Arab men in ragged shorts, bare chests, and a strong inclination to scratch. It was a vivid and startlingly beautiful spot.

One of the ways I have been helping Gay is by taking care of her six-year-old daughter, Sheila. I give her showers, have her take naps in my bed, watch her on deck, and help her with her meals. It is fun doing this and I know I shall love being a mother if I am ever lucky enough. In the mornings, she dashes into my room now, still in her little nightgown, and it is great fun to have an early morning kiss and conversation. She pours my tea for me and presents it to me when I am still in bed. She adores my doll, Natasha, (just like the dolls I sent to Helen, Pat, and Jean) whom I bought the day before I left Germany. She thinks Natasha talks, and we have many a whispered conversation among the three of us—Natasha, Sheila, and I. One great criticism I have for the English is the way they do everything for their children. I am certainly going to have my daughter dressing herself by the time she is five. Gay didn't tell Sheila that her father had been killed for the first few days. But yesterday, Sheila came for her morning visit and said, "My father is in Paradise." We've had several talks about Paradise since then, and I find it pretty hard since I am not at all convinced that there is such a place. Sheila has decided that though it may be very nice for her father, she certainly doesn't want to go there herself for some time, or have her mother go, either.

7 January 1950—Bay of Bengal, entering the Straits of Malacca

Tomorrow we arrive in Singapore! Gay, Jo Rackham, Mrs. Warren and Peggy will leave the *Mongolia* here, and after a three day visit the rest of us will sail onto Siam. In a way, it will be quite nice to have us an even smaller and cozier group. To be rid of Mrs. W. will be the biggest blessing of our trip.

This stretch across the Indian Ocean and the Bay of Bengal has been both horrible and wonderful. The "horrible" has been the agony which Gay has suffered. I really believe that I have helped her live through this, and I can't express what that means to me. To find a woman in the greatest conceivable pain and to help diminish that pain is a wonderful, wonderful thing. It helps me to believe that all of the suffering I went through was for some good if I can use what I learned then to make another person happier now.

Gay and I have had many talks out on the lifeboat at night, far up at the bow of the ship, and in her cabin and mine. Part of the talks have just been about life in Burma, in China, and in Singapore. It is fantastic the things an Englishwoman who has lived in the East takes for granted. Shootings, snakes, guards, sudden death, jungle magic, etcetera, are as common to Gay as cornflakes and movies are to an American. And yet when she hears of me driving around Europe alone, she is weak with admiration at my courage. I just can't understand it.

One thing which I can never live with is the colossal, blanketing prejudice which the English have for "colored" people. Italians, Spanish, Anglo-Indians—all count as "colored" to Gay. Even brown eyes are something she looks upon with suspicion. It goes without saying what she thinks of Jews. And the more I talk to her the more amazed I am at her reasons for her compete refusal to accept any of these people as equals.

I hope that I, myself, am not being prejudiced, but I believe that an American is as open-minded, subject to persuasion, ready to listen and change, and is as eager to meet each situation with the proper solution as is anybody in the world. (What an unwieldy sentence.) What I am trying to say is that tradition is not an iron vise to shut off all new ideas. We see a situation and we wonder what the best solution is. We do not think about our six hundred-year-old family and do as our ancestors would have done.

These Englishmen have been utterly darling to me, and I think they like me as much as I like them. They are so convinced that Britain is the ultimate in everything that they make the average American look as though he is unpatriotic. But, what I want to say is that I am thrilled to the core that I belong to a young, polyglot, thriving, changing country. I'd suffocate as an Englishwoman, or would at least end up friendless, for I would never consider Merle Oberon as "colored" and slave-like just because she is the child of an Englishman and an Indian. If I fall in love with an Indian, I shall certainly marry him. This may cause me to miss the friendship of the English who will scorn me from the bottom of their souls. It is just that I cannot imagine such traditional English thinking to help in making an interesting person. They live by a strange code which seems to follow ancient rules more than common sense.

Peggy Deans is the great exception. She and I have been having wonderful talks every morning. We lie in the sun on top of a lifeboat and talk from nine until noon every day. She is a darling, liberal, brave soul. She is thirty-five, I believe, and she is heart-broken that she has waited so long for this adventure. She said last night that when you have a wonderful time all at once, you wonder why you didn't start living like this ten years sooner.

I thought about my last ten years, and I realized that there were very few things in them which I would change. This is a glorious way to feel about one's life, and I owe this to our father, Dockie and his spirit of curiosity.

Last night I sat up on the lifeboat and it looked the way the Bay of Bengal ought to look. The sea was dark, turbulent, white-capped. The sky was filled with huge, threatening clouds. Every now and then there were open patches of sky sprinkled with stars. A strong, warm, salty wind was blowing, and then suddenly from low on the water a huge, rounded, golden moon appeared. It was a dark night and yet a light one. I could see clouds and stars and moon and waves. The wind was ripping at my hair and clothes until I thought I would lose them all. It was fierce and tigerish and exactly the atmosphere which you would associate with the vivid word "Bengal."

By now, I have a most delectable suntan. I think it is the best I have ever had. I am a deep bronze from head to toe with very few exceptions. I have gained at least five pounds and I sleep almost eleven hours a night, so it would be hard for anyone to feel better in the entire world.

Peggy and I covered the ship yesterday and the day before, taking pictures of each other. It is about time I had some pictures taken of me, for I have always been the girl behind the camera. We went from the bow to the poop deck to the bridge and I think the results should be pretty exciting. We also took some of us sunbathing on the lifeboat. These moments are almost my favorite, for I lie there utterly relaxed, with the spray and sun and wind whipping over me, and when I open my eyes I see only ship and sea. I feel I could continue this journey forever and ever and never be bored or tired or unhappy.

Singapore will hold both happiness and sorrow. Much of the time I will spend with Gay, and that will be pretty hard. Some of the time I'm going on my own, however, and for one evening, Peggy and I are stepping out. I have vowed to myself to have a Singapore Sling from the bar of the Raffles Hotel, and I shall have one, come hell or high water. I announced my intention at dinner, and it was very funny to see the expressions. "Nice girls don't go to bars alone"—and though you have come 15,000 miles from home to have this little experience, you just aren't "nice" if you quietly see it through. Thank God I am an American, and that my feelings of right and wrong stem from reason, not habit.

January 1950—Singapore

I must make haste to get down on paper at once some of the thrill and excitement and glamour which are running through my being at this moment. In a short time, Peggy, several of the ship's officers, and I are going "out on the town," but I can't bear to leave until I have captured some of the magic of today.

Perhaps the most glorious moment was when footsore, broke, and with blistered palms from the weight of the bag full of bundles I was carrying, I sank into a bicycle-drawn rickshaw. We darted and dashed and curved along the streets of this intriguing city back to the *Mongolia*. I had on a darling scarlet cotton skirt and top, purple Neopolitan sandals, and a huge scarlet and purple cookie hat which I bought today. At my feet was a bag filled with brocades, kimonos, knick-knacks, creams, and old silks. Though my head was whirling with the realization that I was doing this in real life and not in a dream, it was all a hundred times more exciting than I even dared to hope. Whatever comes next, this has been worth it.

Singapore is the photographer's paradise, though I haven't yet taken a picture because I've been so busy just looking and gasping. My rickshaw passed a river full of black-sailed junks, pagoda-style buildings, palms, bananas, and tumbledown store fronts. The natives are Chinese, Malayan, Indian, Egyptian, and mixtures unknown. They wear sarongs, Chinese silks, rag skirts, next-to-nothing, turbans, and coolie hats. Odd combinations are also visible on men wearing business shirts and women in bright cotton skirts.

The smells are strong and sour, but the nursing babies, shimmering sea food, brilliant fruits, vivid rags, and the general filth which contribute to these smells almost make them worthwhile. Each building has several poles jutting from the upstairs windows, and on these poles hang the daily wash. You can imagine how it looks when you see red, green, pink, purple and scarlet shirts, underpants, sarongs, and other garments for blocks and blocks. There are shaven heads, beards, sparse dangling whiskers, gaunt brown legs, slanting eyes, and bare behinds on all sides. It is much like Mexico City in that a great deal of the life is found just squatting on the city streets. I passed men playing dice, cards, shoe-repairing, cooking, sleeping, begging, and spitting—all from a reclining position on the city sidewalks. Remarkable. It is just plain heaven to see, and I fear I shall die of mere happy heart failure!

Last night we docked and Peggy and I took ourselves out. First we headed right for the Raffles Hotel, where we each had a cold and frothy Singapore Sling. Rarely have I felt so touristy and even decadent, for we were so brown, so European looking, so eagerly staring, so obviously where two ladies should not be alone, that no one could have missed us for anything but two girls living through a most juvenile and glorious moment.

Afterwards, we went to a rather smooth night club for dinner and were promptly joined by an eager young Australian pilot. He took us out dancing and amused us very much. Me, because he spoke with a cockney accent, and Peggy because he was so jubilant and boasting and talkative—in other words, *American!* The people in the clubs are mostly English and all dress in white and look too perfectly self-satisfied to believe.

For just plain chic and attractiveness, I think it is hard to beat a group of American women. The Englishwomen collectively will certainly never win a beauty prize. They seem determined to conceal as much as possible the fact that they are female, curved, and soft. They look like spinsters of fifty doing something of which they greatly disapprove.

The interior of the hotels and bars are most unique to someone from America, for they all have overhead electric fans everywhere, many tropical flowers and palms, and the orchestras are small, native string affairs. The lighting is subdued, the coloring in soft golds and muted pastels, and from such a spot you step out into a moon-drenched lawn with tropical palms silhouetted against the night. Any MGM movie you have ever seen about the Far East is pure understatement. This is to be my native habitat from now on.

11 January 1950—in the South China Sea, approaching the Isthmus of Kra

Goodbye to Singapore and three wonderful days—not to mention four nights of dancing, toasting, sight-seeing, and bliss. The days I spent alone, with the exception of one day with Peggy. I wandered through big department stores, into back alleyways, into every shop in Chinatown, and across bridges and narrow roads. I took pictures, though not nearly enough, because it was too exciting just looking to stop and set up my camera.

I did a lot of shopping and hired a rickshaw by the hours. The shops are a woman's paradise. Satin robes, embroidery, silks, laces, native prints, jade earrings, opal bracelets, embroidered brocaded slippers, negligees and frothy nightgowns abound on every counter and are almost always within one's budget. I just could not believe that I could pick and choose among faraway dreams and come home with a bundle full of the Orient just for me.

I am just no good at bargaining. I nearly always pay the price they ask. Strangely enough, they hate you for this, and in one store where I spent nearly all of my money and still did not attempt to bargain, the man finally ended up by giving me a handkerchief—more in disgust at me for being such a poor business woman. I told him that even though he felt he was getting the best of me, I was still so divinely happy with my purchases that I would have been willing to pay more than the asking price for the same things.

I think I have been stared at by the Europeans and natives as much as I have stared at them. That is one thing about Singapore which amazed me. It is really a small town. Faces begin to look familiar in the streets and in the restaurants, and several times I bumped into people I knew from the ship.

I suppose that my nights have been as much fun as anything on this trip. Our second night, Peggy and I went out with two of the ship's officers. Only the Captain, the Chief Engineer, and the Chief Mate are permitted to associate with the passengers. Therefore, it took a long time for us to get to know the Second Mate and the Second Engineer. They are really charming men, and gentlemen to their fingertips. I don't remember how much I have said about Danish men so far, but on the whole they are as good-looking, brawny, courteous, and handsome as any men I have ever seen.

At any rate, Peggy and I strolled to the customs gate to meet the two officers who also strolled there in a nonchalant fashion designed to fool the Captain in case he saw us all together. We hopped into a taxi and off we went to a place called The New World. It is a taxi dance center, and the men were most reluctant to take us there. I have never been to a taxi dance place before, however, and was thrilled and determined to see one in Singapore. It was huge and dark and filled with excellent music. Girls were lined up around the dance floor in chairs and we sat in tables behind them. I really didn't pay much attention to the girls after the first minute, because soon three or four more crew members joined us, and I danced and danced until I ached all over! It was friendly and joyous and fun. Much as I adore the ship, it is also nice to go ashore once in a while.

When The New World closed, we hired taxis and headed for Chinatown. The smell and jumble and weird wailing music which characterizes this place at all times seems especially fantastic and remote at night. As I headed up the stairs of a particularly disreputable-looking place, I felt that almost anything could happen to me once I reached the top of the stairs. It was most reassuring to look back at five huge friendly Danes, and to know that they could certainly take care of themselves and of Peggy and me, no matter what lay in store for us. As it turned out, it was only Chinese food!

The following two nights, I went out alone with the Second Engineer. He is only a year older than I, but seems at least ten years older. He is the youngest officer of his rank (equal to a commander in the Navy) in the East Asiatic maritime world, and proved to be the perfect escort for Singapore. He has a lot of Heathcliff in him, which I managed to resist, since he is a married man and has a most charming and provocative way of speaking English, and a reckless way of spending money which I really enjoyed. (It is not the amount spent which I liked, but the way in which he tossed it on the table with complete indifference to price as long as he got what he wanted.) I can imagine that he has had quite an eventful life in his years at sea. At any rate, he seemed to like me very much and was most adorably complimentary, attentive, thoughtful, and completely respectful of me. I admire a sailor who decides he would rather go ashore with a girl whom he likes to dance with and talk with, knowing that it will be completely platonic, than to get himself some Oriental belle of the Far East and spend the night in bed.

His name is atmospheric enough—Moegens Jorgenson! He and I always meet at the customs gate (with Moegens following me since the harbor-side is no place for a girl to wander around at night). Then we hop into a taxi and head to the Raffles for a drink. The orchestra is soft and dreamy, and so far we seem to be the only people dancing. Both nights the Australian pilot joined us, with absolute adoration in his eyes for me, and making many plans about flying over to Manila.

The first night Mo and I went to a most exotic and glamorous cabaret after the Raffles and danced and danced, plus had a few scotch and sodas and seemingly endless conversation. (One thing I have definitely noticed…the East is no place for drinking. One drink here is worth four in Germany or America. The heat must do something to one's system.) It is fun to talk to Mo, for our ways of life are totally different, and it is just interesting to discuss and to argue and explain. Also, I love to speak English with a man who knows enough of it to be fluent, but who mixes up his words. For example, when he is telling me to be careful, he always says, "Be care, gypsy." I suppose one of the reasons I have been so happy these past days is that I am a bronze-skinned American girl in Singapore with a Danish officer. The whole combination is so carefree and on-the-brink and infinitely reckless. After the cabaret closed we walked for hours. There wasn't a soul in sight on one of those nights—for blocks and blocks—except for the beds which appear all along the sidewalk late in the evening with black-skinned Malayans sleeping on them for coolness.

I knew the way back to the ship, and arm in arm we wandered by the river, in the middle of the street, over weird gullies and gutters, past shuttered store fronts, through deserted squares and down by the ships. It was as though we were the only actors left on a tremendous life-sized movie set of Singapore, except that Singapore is more so than any movie will ever dare paint it. It is the most loosely knit string of Europe, India, and the Far East; richness and incredible poverty; love, vice, and animal spirits and actions; trailing ragged gowns and filmy Indian flowing robes; insistent bells from the rickshaws, droning Chinese chanting, screeching, wailing, screaming children and merchants and women!—I just can't put it all into words. It defies all my descriptions. I can just say that the whole time I was there I moved in a warm, contented, ecstatic dream, holding a satin kimono in a bundle under my arm, scooting through traffic in a rickshaw, hand in hand with a protective, delightful Danish officer, Singapore slings at the Raffles, and moonlight and palms.

I suppose this honeymoon for one which I am on will have to be over someday, but for the moment I feel ready to die just of happiness. I am going to move heaven and earth to stay out in the Far East. Marriage to anyone who isn't planning a life here too looks steadily more unattractive. This trip is making me count my blessings in a manner I have never really experienced before. I feel guilty writing to each of you, because just the way a happily married person thinks no one else knows what life is all about unless he is married, so, too, do I feel that no one is living if he isn't feeling the warmth and rush and magic of the lands beyond the sea. One thing more. There just isn't such a thing as a single white girl out here. I can see that once I meet a few people for a start, my life will be just as social and full and utterly overwhelming as Gay predicted.

18 January 1950—South China Sea—Leaving Siam for Manila

Siam! In a sense, there is no place one is so unlikely to go. No place quite so far away. Therefore, when you suddenly find yourself sunning on a beach, having bacon and eggs at Hotel Trocadero, stopping a rickshaw driver to take a picture of dilapidated houseboats on a small canal, or breathing heavily into a lavender scented handkerchief to get you through the smells of an especially small, hot street, and as you do all of these things, you ask yourself, "Where am I?" Then, when the answer is *Siam*, it is just too impossible to believe. (Once again I say I cannot build a sentence—so please ignore it!)

We arrived at a small island sixty miles from Bangkok late on a Saturday afternoon. It was decided that the ship was too heavily loaded to go up the river to Bangkok and that it would be very expensive, difficult and uncertain for any of the passengers to try to get into the city. Though I was disappointed, I felt that one world capital more or less was rather immaterial.

Saturday night was fun. First, huge coolie-laden rafts were anchored alongside our ship. They were the longshoremen of Siam. They had tiny stoves, rice pots and jugs of water aboard and they would work, eat, and sleep at our side until the *Mongolia* was once again ready to sail.

I was leaning next to the Captain when a small fleet of sampans (I think that is the native name for these tiny rowing boats) well stocked with girls, arrived at the gangway. I have already said that the Captain is about the most terrific specimen of male I ever hope to see.

If you could have seen him lean over the side and bark orders to his men, the women, and the world in general about how we did not want a single woman aboard, it would have made your flesh shrink. Fortunately (or unfortunately) he called out these orders in Danish. The girls, who have visited Danish ships before, answered in Danish, and it must have been quite an exchange. The Second Engineer was standing on the deck above us, and I saw him a few minutes later. His face was scarlet, and he said it was a good thing the passengers couldn't understand Danish. Apparently the Captain, in spite of his exertions, was unable to keep the girls away, for that night the ship was riddled with them. As the Captain would stalk up one ladderway to the poop deck, the girls would creep down the other ladderway. It must have been a hilarious sight, and I bet few people got much rest.

However—enough on that subject. The next day, the Captain led us ashore on a delightful expedition. We walked around a section of old villas and pagodas which had been built for the Emperor of Siam as his summer home. Because of trouble with the French, he never came to live there, and so nobody has ever occupied these mansions except lizards and an occasional squatter. There were marble floors, exotic flower beds, tree-lined paths, crumbling stone stairways, a huge swimming pool, a white pagoda for worship, and villas for all of the ministers of state. Everything was a combination of starkly awesome, and at the same time, it all appeared tumbled, decrepit, and only an echo of the past.

After this jaunt, we had a picnic lunch fit for a king down on the beach. Then we walked a mile or so to a nearby village and stared intensely at the people, and in turn were intensely stared at by them. On the whole, I would say that the Siamese are friendly, handsome, luxuriously lazy, and rather content to spend their lives in a reclining position. I found one of the belles of the previous night and was happily taking her picture when the Captain bellowed forth, "Madame! Why would you flatter that wench? Come on, at once!"

After we had peeked into stores, bedrooms (which means the house, for I think one three-walled bedroom is all any Siamese family lives in), the schoolhouse, and a dance hall, we got into a couple of motorboats and headed across to a small island which was perfect for swimming. It was called Princess Beach, for in the old days a Siamese princess used to come there to swim. It was heavenly fun to swim in cool salt water, lounge on a white sandy beach, and drink cold beer with the Captain and the Prices, and the Second Engineer (whom I think rapidly became persona non grata with the Captain, since he likes to be the only man on the horizon).

It was the end of that glorious day that I suddenly found myself off on a new adventure. The agent at whose home we were swimming suggested that I go up the river to Bangkok in a tug which was leaving that night and would return the following night. After a lot of conversation and pros and cons—with many "cons" from the Second Engineer—I found myself boarding a tug at eight that night, with a small string bag containing toothbrush, sandwiches, camera, a blanket and pillow, and my purse, and wearing dangling earrings, gypsy skirt, Mexican blouse, French peasant shoes, Viennese scarf, and my Lanz velvet jacket. The whole ship waved me off and there I was! A single woman, relatively white, and on a boat with only Siamese men—not one of whom spoke English.

As we left the *Mongolia* behind and started up the river to Bangkok, I began to wonder whether I had attempted more that I could see through. I sat at the back of the tug and watched a smiling boy start a tiny fire in a little brick stove. Then he acted out "eating" to me and asked me to join them. Next, he got a black pot and put rice and water in it. Soon the pot was happily settled on the little stove, the small fire looked most dancing and magical, the night was inky black, and all of the tugmen were sitting around staring at me curiously. I hugged my bundles to me and wondered how Kate Salter ever got herself on a tugboat going up the river to Bangkok, Siam, with absolutely no protection whatsoever.

That night I slept in a small, hot, airless cabin. I kept my clothes on and awoke every half hour or so. Often, I would see a man standing silently in the doorway of my cabin looking in at the American lady. I heard screaming tug whistles and the heavy pounding of our tug engine. Bells seemed to be clanging all the time, and I ached with a combination of fear and exhaustion. It is funny that one little symbol kept me from being too afraid. When I had entered this little cabin which belonged to the young Captain of the tug, I had seen there was no lock, no nothing for comfort or protection, and was really very worried about what the night would bring. Then, I spied a can of Yardley's talcum powder on the sink and I decided that where there was Yardley's, there was safety!

We arrived in Bangkok at six-thirty the following morning. I hastily climbed ashore and spent the next two hours sitting on the front veranda of the customs office waiting for a man named Mr. Will, who was supposed to tell me what to do next. It was really very interesting to watch morning come to the waterfront of Bangkok. Tugs, launches, sampans, motor boats, steamers moved up and down the river, barefoot men and women shuffled past the customs office, a small Siamese-style hot dog stand opened up next door and soon was doing a rousing business. Young laborers shoved huge logs over the dockside and laced them into a raft below to be taken down to a waiting ship. Everybody seemed to do a terrific amount of spitting and staring, and finally Mr. Will arrived.

It was soon arranged that I should spend the day in a rickshaw, and Mr. Will told the driver to show me the city, to take me shopping, to the Trocadero for breakfast, to some other huge hotel for lunch, and to contact the company at about one-thirty that afternoon. And away we went!

I hope I'm up to describing Bangkok. It is quite a bit like Singapore, except both richer and poorer. There are canals everywhere with miserable raft-like houses being poled up and down or just parked along the shore. Everybody seems to wear his only clothes and sit or lie or do business on the spot which is his. The traffic is fantastic. Especially when you are a backseat driver sitting in an open little carriage with trucks, busses, cars, and other rickshaws rushing past you, missing you by centimeters, blowing horns, tooting sirens, jingling bells and such. Loudspeakers shrieked out the wailing, chanting Chinese music. Hawkers cried out notice of their strange Oriental wares. Little boys made clicking, drum-like noises on small black castanets to attract attention to the hair ribbons, chestnuts, or combs which they had for sale. Women sprawled in doorways with naked babies. People laughed, argued, stared, whistled, and *smelled*! My rickshaw boy darted and whisked and whizzed through traffic. He didn't know a word of English, so my repeated admonition "Be careful" meant nothing to him and I finally gave up.

After a luxurious scrubbing in the lady's room of the Trocadero and a breakfast of bacon and eggs, I started out for the temples and the palace—not without noticing that I put the entire European population of the dining room in an uproar. There just are not any spare white women out here, and when the men see one, they nearly knock each other over in their anxiety to establish first contact.) Of course, maybe I should not wear the clothes I do, but they feel so right that I just cannot switch to a tailored dress and high-heeled shoes.

I suppose the first glimpse of a Thai palace—no matter how many movies you may have seen about Siam—is something no American will ever forget. All of a sudden you see the pagoda-shaped roofs ablaze with golden, turquoise, rose, silver, scarlet, pink, purple, blue glints. Walls surround the lower ramparts, but the sun glistens so brilliantly on the golden tiles, the millions of stones set mosaically beneath these glimmering roofs, that you feel that you couldn't stand the splendor of seeing the entire structure at once. Fortunately, I had color film in my Leica, and I should have some glorious pictures.

I wandered around all of the courtyards that I could get into. I saw a golden reclining Buddha which must have been about two hundred feet long; I smelled incense in temples; I dropped *ticals* (Siamese money) into charity boxes; I searched in vain for an English-speaking guide who could tell me about what I was seeing; I stared at the Monks dressed in vivid saffron robes, and I marveled at the combination of the fairy castles with the miserable filth and dirt which lived absolutely against the walls of this splendor. On one hand everything is so terribly plush and overwhelming and ornate, and in the same glance you see the nakedness, rags, incredible dirt, and the want of the man on the street. It is much more jumbled together than the Catholic churches of Mexico with the peasants outside. Here, the peasants seem to find a cozy corner right in the church and lie down in it.

I walked, I drove, I shopped, I lunched, I met a friend of the Prices, and finally I arrived at the East Asiatic Shipping Company. I was greeted by a lot of handsome young Danes who told me that I had missed my ride to the ship and might not have a chance to get there at all. You can't imagine the state of mind this caused within my hitherto tranquil interior! I had about sixty dollars left, which would hardly be enough to see me to Manila by air or another ship. There was a tug I could take that night, but it was highly problematical as to whether or not it would reach the *Mongolia* before she left the following morning. However, there was no other way out, so I decided that I would just trust my luck—which so far seems incredibly good, knock on wood!—One of the Danes sent me to his home to spend the remaining part of the afternoon there.

His home was a huge villa. His wife, Inge, was an adorable Danish girl of twenty-one. They had six servants, tennis court, and beautiful gardens. First, I had a bath, and never have I relished anything quite so much. Then, she and I had orangeade, much conversation, and she showed me all around the mansion. The interior was all done in teakwood; the ceilings were so high you could hardly see them. Everywhere were open doors, mosquito netting, overhead electric fans, old carved chests, and quiet servants waiting to do your bidding. This life is certainly a luxurious one, which is pretty far removed from a democratic way of living.

The man, Gunnar Schmidt, came home around five, bringing a couple of strapping young Danes with him. We all had a beer or two, then tea and pancakes, and much conversation. They get so few outsiders here that when one comes in, they really cherish you. After they left, the Schmidts and I had curry and rice, and I was whisked off to the tug. This time, I asked to be allowed to sleep outdoors. It had been too insufferably hot and airless on the tug the night before. Gunnar fixed up a cot for me right on the bridge of the ship. He told the Captain to get me to the *Mongolia* as fast as possible. I waved them off, climbed up the ladder to the bridge, and lay down on my cot with my purse and camera under the blanket with me. It was quite an experience to lie under the open stars, to see the lights of the river boats, the shadowy figures of the tugmen, to see the white-robed night watchman staring down at me from the wharf, and to keep saying over softly to myself that I was in Bangkok, Siam, and in a few hours I might find out that I was staying in Siam just because my beloved ship had already left for Manila.

I just could not face the horror of what it would be like if the *Mongolia* had sailed. For one thing, I have been hoarding these last few days as rare treasures. I want to drain the last bit of sea and sun and comfort from every second, and I couldn't bear to have them all whisked away from me. I lay for more than two hours waiting for the tug to leave. It was a nightmare, for it takes twelve hours to get to the outer island. Every hour was critical.

At last there was a burst of activity. The Captain came up to the bridge, he rang a few bells, and with a clatter of engines, we were off. A few hundred yards down the dockside we pulled up beside a tremendous red raft which was loaded with coolies. They were lying all over the deck, talking, singing, playing cards, munching on bread, and waiting to be towed down to the ships to unload a new one. We finally got them tied to us, and off we went. The worst thing about my position was that I was only two feet from the horn. You have no idea how loud it is, and all night long I would be well-nigh shot out of my bed by the painful roar of that demon. My ears still hurt.

I didn't really sleep at all. I was dead tired. I was happy. I was a bit tense about my future. But most of all, I was thanking my fairy Godmother for the adventure I had been having. To lie flat on your back looking up at the heavens is always an experience to be cherished, but when it is from the bridge of a tug boat and it is in Siam, then, indeed, the "cup runneth over."

For hours we were held up by tides and other boats. Oh! How long it seemed! How dirty I felt! How tired! How frantic I would have been if we should have missed my ship! At last, after I had watched dawn break along the river, I stood up and looked in front of me. There lay the shadow figures of the ships anchored at sea. I got out my binoculars and started searching for the *Mongolia*. This ordeal lasted for more than an hour. I finally found her, only to see her start out to sea! I was almost hysterical by now but no one spoke English, so it did no good.

Finally, at nearly ten o'clock, we were close enough to see that she was still there. But the coolies were gone! This doesn't mean anything to you, but to me it meant the ship was waiting just for me, and the Captain would have plenty to say about it. (It has been a standing joke among the passengers that we would rather miss the ship than to hold it up and have to face the Captain.) I looked through the glasses and there he was on the bridge, looking through his glasses at me. I waved. He did not. Boy, oh boy! Then he hooted the horn of the

Mongolia twelve times, meaning HURRY! They sent a launch out after me, and with blanket, string bag, camera, and all, I scooted aboard the launch and was off to my beloved ship.

Passengers, crew, ship's officers, and stewards were all on hand to watch me climb aboard. I didn't know whether to throw myself down and kiss the deck, I was so happy to see it—or whether I would have been better off had I been left on shore. After a shower and cold-creaming and sinking into my bed, I finally sent the Captain a note. It was a short little thing and the gist of it was "What do I do now? Wait for you to call me, or come to you?" He sent back word that he would see me at lunch. He has had a sore back for days and hasn't been down for any meals, so this was an event in itself.

I think I should say here that it was the Captain who decided to let me go on this outing. The trip had been outlined to me, the dangers of missing the ship, the lack of comfort, etcetera. I had turned to him and said, "What would you do?" He had replied that as Captain of the ship he must tell me that I would be going without his permission. As a person, though, he went on to say that he would not miss a chance to see Bangkok. So—I went.

This Captain has little or no use for women, but I think he likes me. (It may be that he pretends to, or that he has to keep up a front because I am perhaps doing a story, or—I don't know.) I think that he has a certain respect for the way in which I get around and take care of myself. Also I think he, and everybody else on board, is very grateful for the way I took care of Gay O'Neil, because it made it a thousand times easier for all the rest of them.

So, as I put the final touches of perfume on before lunch, I really had my heart in my throat. I heard his voice in the corridor and I popped out. If he were going to give me hell, I would rather have it done privately. I called to him and he turned around, grinning from ear to ear. "Oh no, Madame. You are in disgrace." But, that smile! Never have I been so glad to see someone. During lunch, we had much teasing, laughter, beer, and fun. I think he was delighted with the whole situation, and I think that the *Mongolia* really had to wait only about thirty minutes at the most—which was not, after all, serious.

Later in the afternoon, as I was sitting on the lifeboat, he called me up to the bridge and asked me to tell him about Bangkok. We sat up there in the open sun and talked for nearly two hours. It was amusing and stimulating and interesting. He tells a glorious story, and he has a million to tell. He wanted to hear all of my impressions (he had lived in Siam for two years), and he wanted to give me advice. He said that he always admired a person who seized an adventure when it came his way, but that person should never inconvenience other people by doing so. He was right about this and I told him how sorry I was. Then he started telling me about his adventures, and it was supper time before I left. Last night I slid into bed so happy and so weary that I could no longer think.

Today is Wednesday. Saturday, we arrive in Manila and these next hours I spend having final interviews, taking final pictures, eventually packing, but most of all sitting in the sun, looking at this calm, blue sea, and loving the *Mongolia*.

I have forgotten to mention two things. I have seen a shark twice! Once, in the Indian Ocean, and once, yesterday, when we were talking on the bridge. There are lots of porpoises who frolic at the side of the ship, but a shark is a rare thing to see. It is huge, stately, sinister. Both times it stuck only a small part of its fin above water, but both times the horror of what lay beneath made my imagination see the entire beast. The second thing is that there are millions of flying fish skimming along the top of the sea. These are like darling little humming birds and most restful and fanciful to see.

My new and favorite spot for sitting is at the very tip of the bow of the ship. Where the two sides join together, there is a small strip of metal just my size, and I can lie here and see nothing but clear blue sea ahead, and the length of the entire ship behind. It is the most private, the most exciting, and the most relaxing spot in the world, and I am truly in heaven when I stretch out on my towel and think about all the wonderful things I have to think about, or just not think at all, but feel. It is glorious to be alive, and my luck has been too good. Maybe I'll have to earn it in the unknown life which lies ahead of me when we dock in Manila, on Saturday, the 21st of January, 1950.

My last evening on the *Mongolia,* I had worn a luscious red satin dress which I'd had made just for my last evening on shipboard. With my beautiful garnets and my deep tan, it was really an ensemble to end all ensembles. I had cocktails with the Second Engineer before our regular cocktail party, and he seemed absolutely overwhelmed. He told me—among other things—that in his years of sailing I am the first woman traveling alone who behaved herself for the entire trip. He also murmured a lot of sweet nothings about how he had fallen in love with me, and how the entire ship had, and how much the Captain adored me, all of which was music to hear—although to be taken with much salt. I am glad to say that I did behave myself on the trip, and that the only romance I had was with the sea itself.

I found out that the Captain had earlier made a special three-hour trip by motor boat to meet me when I returned from Bangkok (although I returned a different way and so his trip was in vain), and the main reason the *Mongolia* waited for me was that it was the Captain's special desire to have Miss Salter aboard again. I say all of these things not out of conceit, but because of the warm delight I feel that the ardent love I had for the whole adventure was returned in part by the people with whom I sailed. The Prices gave a cocktail party for me the last night. The Captain appeared for dinner, which he has not done for weeks. And, on the last morning, the Captain invited me to the bridge to have cocktails with him in his cabin.

On the last night, I went up to the bridge just to look at the night and to see the last sight of ocean, spray, masts, and fresh sea winds, which I shall not experience again for quite a while. I could have wept with my sorrow at leaving, if it were not for the fact that I was landing in Manila and about to begin an entirely new adventure. If my destination had been the USA and some quiet town in the Midwest, I believe I would have preferred to just die of joy on the bridge of the *Mongolia* in the midst of the magic environment of ship and sea.

22 January 1950—Manila, the Philippines

This last entry should really have been written yesterday morning as we sailed into the harbor of Manila, but at that time,

I was so absolutely overwhelmed with nervous excitement that writing was a complete impossibility.

The *Mongolia* sails on to Hong Kong sometime today and Cabin G will no longer belong to Miss Salter. Never have I been so loathe to leave a home as at the moment Dockie and I walked down the gangway to the dock below. All of the sailors were on hand to wave me off, and the Second Engineer and the young boy who gave me the Christmas present both looked almost tearful. It was a most heavenly experience, and I think that the obvious appreciation which I had for it endeared me to nearly all of the Danes on the ship.

My trip on the freighter is over. I suppose it has been a dream of at least fifteen years to take such a trip, and now that I have it tucked away in my memory, I can say that it was worth fifteen years of dreaming. It was a perfect experience. My whole being is so tired now with just the aftermath of excitement that I can't find the exact words to thank life which has given me this treasure.

Dockie and I live in a tropical place which looks very promising. Dockie himself is utterly charming, the packet of mail awaiting me promises all sorts of wonderful things for the future, and what is to come next may very well live up to this miracle of perfection which I have just completed.

12 January 1950—University of Philippines

Just as I began this document with "Well my darlings," so do I end it. Here is the final page. My journal is long and perhaps dull to those of you who were not with me. But read it when and if you feel like it. It is too expensive to send via air mail, so it will probably be February before you get it. By then, I should have written several personal letters to each of you. It was perfectly wonderful to hear from those of you who wrote along the way, and I give each correspondent a million thanks. The others of you are scoundrels—except that it was such fun to write to you, too.

Love,
Kate

Kate, bottom left, pictured with
students in her English class in Manila

A thoughtful Kate at the end of her voyage

Afterword

My mother, Kate, spent six months after her *Mongolia* voyage with her father, Dockie, in Manila, who was a visiting Fulbright Scholar at the University of the Philippines. After teaching a summer school English course there, Kate returned to the Pentagon where she resumed her position working for the Office of War Information, liaising with national reporters and authors whose articles on the war were featured in department publications. Her position level was the equivalent of a lieutenant colonel, giving her authority to take some creative license for originating feature stories on the war. Through this job, she became acquainted with editors and reporters for *LIFE* magazine.

In December 1951 Kate met her future husband, Sayed Ahmed Mahmood. He was attending engineering school at Fort Belvoir, Virginia. An omniscient fortune teller who had earlier told Kate she would marry a "tall, dark, handsome foreigner" was indeed prescient. In June 1952 she accepted a position with *LIFE* magazine and moved to New York City. Sayed was clearly concerned and dismayed, recognizing he might lose Kate to her new career with the renowned magazine. He followed her to New York City and promptly proposed to her.

Because she adored her coveted job at *LIFE*, it was with a somewhat heavy heart she left her post to join Sayed in Pakistan. She realized that prospects of a future family and life with Sayed were her priority, so with an open mind and heart, she boldly set forth for this new foreign frontier.

She spent the next fourteen years living in Pakistan as she and my father, Sayed raised a family of five children, two from his previous marriage and three of their own. Mother was actively involved in volunteer work with the Hospice in Pakistan and with the Holy Family Hospital. She played an integral role teaching natural childbirth to expectant mothers, recognizing the value of this in a third world country.

With the tragic death of Sayed in a car accident on Christmas Eve 1965, Kate's life was interrupted again. Although many a woman could become despondent and weighed down by the burden and hardship facing widowhood, this was not the case for my mother. In a letter to her sisters she alluded to her strength: "I feel so fulfilled and complete and loved that I glow, even in widowhood, and this is because my last fifteen years have been so wonderfully right… All the more when there are children who need you so and love you so."

The decision to return to America with her family became paramount. With a nominal amount of currency and an extraordinary amount of courage and fortitude, she returned with her children to the United States in 1966. After working as a schoolteacher in Hamden, Connecticut, she launched a successful twenty-year career in real estate. True to her middle name, Katharine *Shepard* Salter, she did indeed shepherd her family along, providing a sound and solid foundation for each child to pursue their own journey and achieve meaningful vocations. Her personal sense of purpose and the realization that she had exceeded her own expectations for travel and adventure early in life enabled her to be an extraordinary beacon of light and love. Her home was always a "house of spirits," offering a convivial atmosphere and shelter to many. The photographs, oriental rugs, twinkling lamps, relics and remnants from the Far East suffused our house with an elegant clutter that welcomed many a foreign friend traveling abroad. Laughter and good humor permeated our entire home as she would regale friends and family alike with her exotic tales. These are memories I will always cherish.

After the sad death of her beloved step-daughter Faerial from cancer, Kate left Connecticut and spent the last seven years of her life in Zurich, Switzerland with me, my husband, Philipp, and our daughter, Natalia. Although her mantra was often that her rich memories would carry her anywhere in life, the painful fact that she would be robbed of even these memories due to the onset Alzheimer's was regrettable indeed.

Our family's initial response to observing the disease slowly erase her memory was to read aloud from the lovely onionskin letters she had saved, carefully recounting each and every event of her MS *Mongolia* voyage. She always had a broad smile on her face, as each recollection seemed to ignite an ember of fading memory.

In her final years it became evident that she had an uncanny ability to live in the present. A light gust of wind on her face, the dawn of a new day, a stroll along the lake, and the comfort of her family were what she coveted most. She was a person who lived her life to the fullest, and always faced adversity with the belief that all was possible. She did not simply dream her dreams, she boldly lived them. This remarkable talent for accepting what "is" with such grace and dignity allowed her to live to the venerable age of eighty-seven.

Kashya Mahmood Hildebrand

Boarding in Antwerp

Kate, third from right, with shipmates

Kate's cabin porthole

On her favourite perch

Kate with First Mate Pedersen

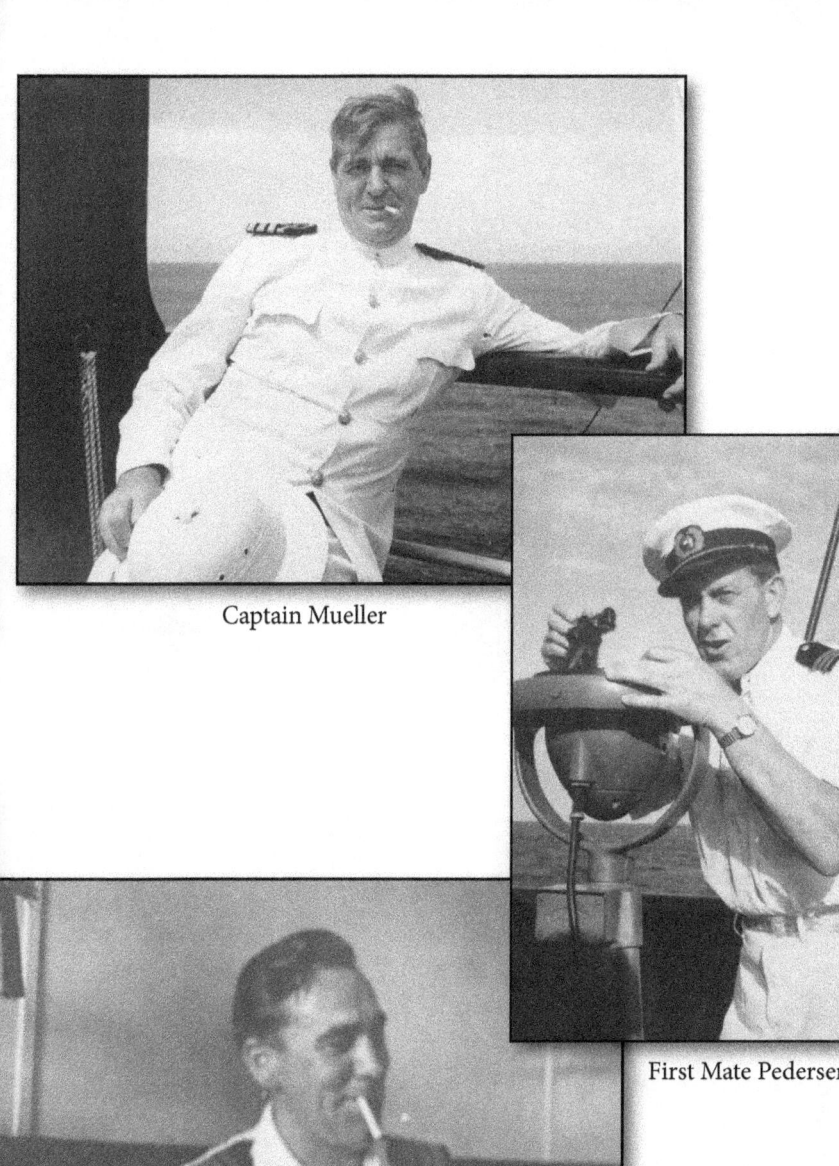

Captain Mueller

First Mate Pedersen

Second Engineer Moegens Jorgenson

Kate with the Third Officer

Kate wins the helm

Kate with a crew member

A cool morning on board the MS *Mongolia*

Arriving to Port at Aden

Bargaining in Aden

Kate with a cabin boy

On the Indian Ocean

Kate in Singapore

Rickshaw taxi ride in Singapore

Coming into Manila Bay

Dockie waving as the ship arrives in Manila

Kate at her desk at *LIFE* magazine in 1952

Kate sets sail from New York Harbor to join Sayed in Pakistan.

Kate enjoying solitude

Kate with her future husband,
Sayed Mahmood, in Washington

www.ingramcontent.com/pod-product-compliance
Lightning Source LLC
Chambersburg PA
CBHW051653040426
42446CB00009B/1114